More Praise for
Through, With, & In Him

Shane Kapler, in *Through, With, & In Him*, opens the eyes of the reader to the value of prayer. One comes away with the tools for an ever-deepening relationship with Christ. At a time when few people pray every day, this new book will enhance one's prayer life as Jesus leads us closer to the Father.

ARCHBISHOP ROBERT CARLSON, St. Louis, MO

Shane Kapler has reflected deeply upon the Scriptures and the history of the Christian people. He make it clear that the mystery of God is not something to be figured out, but rather something to immerse oneself in.

BISHOP THOMAS J. PAPROCKI, Springfield, IL

I am excited about this book. It is practical, very informative, and flexible. I hope it will be widely read because it can truly help people who wonder how to pray, or how to pray better.

FR. JAMES KUBICKI, National Director of the
Apostleship of Prayer, author of *A Heart On Fire:
Rediscovering Devotion to the Sacred Heart of Jesus*

Shane Kapler has done it again. *Through, With, & In Him* beautifully and masterfully demonstrates that when our eyes are opened to the rich theological truths of the Church, seen through their ancient Jewish scriptural and liturgical roots, our hearts will stand all the more ready to embrace that Sacred Heart of Christ who taught us to how to pray.

DR. KEVIN VOST, author of *Memorize The Faith!*
and *From Atheism to Catholicism*

Through, With, & In Him opens us to the startling reality of our continuous participation in Jesus's eternal prayer. This richly textured book takes us from our incorporation into the divine family to our sharing in Jesus's Resurrection. Readers might just find themselves praying their way through it.

BERT GHEZZI, author of *Adventures in Daily Prayer*

Shane Kapler is a gifted writer with extraordinary insight. *Through, With, & In Him* combines this insight with a highly relatable style that makes this book a joy to read. He shines a light on the richness of the prayer life of Jesus and ably demonstrates why it is relevant to our lives today.

KEVIN LOWRY, COO of the Coming Home
Network, author of *Faith At Work*

A pioneering, theological investigation into the soul of him who saved the world. Shane Kapler has opened wide the doors to the spiritual life of THE spiritual master. I highly recommend this magnificent work for anyone who desires more in their relationship with Christ.

JARED ZIMMERER, author of *Man Up!
Becoming the New Catholic Renaissance Man*

Shane Kapler gives us brilliant insights into the prayer life of Jesus and how we can become better pray-ers through, with and in Jesus and his Church. His book takes you on a journey through thousands of years of relationship building between God and His people, and lays out a simple, yet profound plan for each of us to grow closer to God through prayer. I highly recommend it.

JOHN LABRIOLA, author of *Onward Catholic Soldier*

Thoroughly fascinating and enlightening, *Through, With, & In Him* is an exceedingly practical teaching tool which utilizes Scripture and history and sheds light on centuries-old prayers and devotions to help us discover the way to enter into Jesus's prayer.

DONNA-MARIE COOPER O'BOYLE, EWTN TV host, author of
The Miraculous Medal: Stories, Prayers, and Devotions
and *Mother Teresa and Me: Ten Years of Friendship*

Shane Kapler's *Through, With, & In Him* is at once both inspiring and informative. I was amazed by his knowledge of the Israelites' prayer and worship, as well as his insights into their connection with Jesus and the New Covenant. This book shows you step-by-step how to deepen your own prayer life and make Jesus your model for praying.

DEVIN ROSE, author of *If Protestantism
is True: The Reformation Meets Rome*

THROUGH, WITH, & IN HIM

Shane Kapler

THROUGH, WITH, & IN HIM

The Prayer Life of Jesus & How to Make It Our Own

✝

Foreword by
KEVIN VOST

Introduction by
MIKE AQUILINA

Angelico Press

First published in the USA by Angelico Press
© Shane Kapler 2014
Foreword © Kevin Vost 2014
Introduction © Mike Aquilina 2014

ISBN 978-1-62138-055-9 (pbk: alk. paper)

Cover image: James Tissot (French, 1836–1902)
The Communion of the Apostles (La communion des apôtres), 1886–1894.
Brooklyn Museum, Purchased by public subscription, *00.159.223*
Cover design: Cristy Deming

DEDICATION

This book is dedicated to the many people who have
taken me deeper into the prayer life of Jesus,
foremost among them:

My first prayer partners—
my father and mother, Daniel and Nancy Kapler

Extraordinary youth ministers—
Paul Masek, Mary Beth Chik,
and Bill and Ruth Patty

And three men who exemplify
the priesthood of Jesus Christ—
Fathers John Wetmore, Dale Wunderlich,
and John Leykam

ACKNOWLEDGMENTS

First and foremost I must thank my good friend, Dr. Kevin Vost. Kevin was the first person I spoke to of this project, and he was an untiring source of encouragement and support all the way through to its publication. This work would not have seen the light of day without him. I am also completely indebted to Michael and Heather Vento, who prayed for its success, invited me over for many dinners, and patiently listened to early drafts being read aloud. My sincere thanks also go to Denise Fath, a tremendous young theologian, and Katie Gilbert, a dear friend and literature teacher, for their generosity in reading the manuscript and offering such helpful suggestions.

Finally, allow me to express my deep gratitude to Dr. Scott Hahn, whose work has inspired and shaped me, and Joseph Cardinal Ratzinger—our Pope Emeritus, Benedict—to whose scholarship these pages owe so much.

Nihil Obstat:
Reverend John P. Cush, S.T.L.
Diocesan Censor

Imprimatur: Most Reverend Nicholas DiMarzio, Ph.D., D.D.
Bishop of Brooklyn, October 31, 2012

(The Nihil Obstat and Imprimatur are the Church's declarations that a work is free from error in matters of faith and morals. It in no way implies that the Church endorses the contents of the work.)

CONTENTS

Foreword

In His manner of living our Lord gave an example of perfection
as to all those things which of themselves relate to salvation.
⁓ St. Thomas Aquinas, *Summa Theologica*, III, Q. 40, art. 2.

Shane Kapler has taught me a great deal about Christ's love
through his book *The God Who is Love*, through his *Explaining
Christianity* blog posts, and through his many earnest and eloquent
Catholic radio appearances. I have learned even more, though, by
having been blessed to call him my colleague and my friend. I have
seen firsthand how Shane radiates good cheer and Christian charity
in his interactions with me, my family, his family, food servers at
restaurants, young student volunteers at St. Joseph Radio—in sum,
with everyone he meets. I think he does this so well because he sees
Christ in all of us and because he so effectively allows Christ to love
through, with, and in him.

The "Him" of the *Through, With, and In Him* title is Christ Himself, of course. Shane has diligently researched and prayerfully med-
itated upon the roots, stem, fruits, and flowers of the prayer life of
Jesus Christ, and he shows us in these pages how to plant such
prayer within our own hearts. It is a special treat and honor, therefore, to write a brief foreword to Shane's newest great work of love.

This foreword is intended as the direct opposite of a forewarning,
as a few words that say *not* "Watch out for dangers ahead!" but that
say "Watch out for deep and joyous insights that lie in wait in the
forthcoming pages!" "Watch out, lest you find yourself thinking of
Christ more often, loving him more deeply, and praying more fer-
vently in the very ways that he showed us!" Unfortunately, I can't
think of a word conveying just that meaning that starts with the
prefix "fore." "Foretaste" is a possible candidate. I do hope to build

your anticipation, but have neither the space nor the ability to give you much of an appetizing sample of the spiritual feast laid out within the chapters to come. The closest thing to my intention is the two-word phrase "Forward march!"

I will get out of the way then and let you march forth into these pages, for Shane Kapler has done it again. *Through, With, and In Him* beautifully and masterfully demonstrates that when our eyes are opened to the rich theological truths of the Church, seen through their ancient Jewish scriptural and liturgical roots, our hearts will stand all the more ready to embrace that Sacred Heart of Christ who taught us to how to pray.

Thank you, Shane, and bless you, reader. Sweet lessons of Christ await you.

KEVIN VOST
Springfield, Illinois
November 15, 2013
Feast of St. Albert the Great

Introduction

by Mike Aquilina

✝

OUR RELATIONSHIP with God—like all our personal relationships—involves our whole person. God created human beings out of dust, yet breathed into each of us a spiritual life (Gen. 2:7). We are composed of body and soul, and made in the image and likeness of God (Gen. 1:27). The Catholic tradition engages the whole person in prayer, the body as well as the soul, the intellect as well as the emotions. When we meet a friend or acquaintance, we communicate not only with words, but also by the way we dress for the occasion, by the way we comport ourselves, by the places where we choose to meet. Such things matter when we meet God in prayer. It is not only our souls that pray. *We pray*—with our bodies, too.

Jesus prayed this way. His prayer and his person were so united that they are practically indistinguishable. In his book *Behold the Pierced One*, Cardinal Joseph Ratzinger (later Pope Benedict XVI) said, "[P]rayer was the central act of the person of Jesus and, indeed, . . . this person is constituted by the act of prayer, of unbroken communication with the one he calls 'Father.'" The cardinal concluded, "We see who Jesus is if we see him at prayer."

The eternal Son of God did not need to take flesh in order to pray. He has been communicating with the Father from all eternity. He assumed a human nature in order to show us how to live a human life.

He prayed always. He prayed without ceasing. But his prayer wasn't a constant improvisation. It wasn't just free-form. In fact, it took very specific forms. Jesus observed the liturgy of the Jews. He went to synagogue every Sabbath, and he made pilgrimage to Jerusalem on the major feast days. Sometimes he went off by himself to pray in deserted places; and sometimes he prayed in the company of his friends. He observed the solemn ritual meals of his religion. He read the Scriptures. He recited the Psalms. He fasted. He used the traditional morning prayer "Hear, O Israel. . . ."

Jesus led a sustained and disciplined life of prayer. He prayed spontaneously, but he also kept the pious practices that the Jews of his time had inherited from their ancestors. Again, he did not *need* to do any of this. He did it so that we could see what a life of prayer should look like.

Our prayer life, too, needs to take on a certain form so that we're living prayer as Jesus did, with its various expressions and themes and forms. To that end, spiritual masters advise us to develop a "plan of life" or "program of life," a firm but flexible program that schedules our times of focused prayer amid the ordinary duties of work, family life, and social life.

Some people avoid routines of prayer because they would like their relationship with God to be marked by spontaneity. But spontaneity and regularity are not mutually exclusive. Jesus's life included both ritual prayer and extemporaneous prayer. The formulas of traditional prayer give us words and phrases that perfectly express the conditions of our own souls and the circumstances of our lives. But those words won't occur to us unless we have made them our own through repetition.

And that brings me to the book you are holding: It gives more than most of us know how to wish for. By exploring the human prayer of Jesus and how it is continued within the life of the Church, Shane Kapler leads readers beyond "prayers" to prayer. By beginning to pray in the way described here, we can begin to live our heaven even as we pass our days on earth. As the child's voice said to St. Augustine: "Take up and read!" This book can change your life for the better.

Preface

As [Jesus] was praying, the appearance of his countenance was altered, and his clothing became dazzling white. And behold, two men talked with him, Moses and Elijah, who appeared in glory and spoke of his exodus, which he was to accomplish at Jerusalem.

~ Luke 9:29–31

PUT YOURSELF in the shoes of Peter, James, and John for a moment. Jesus invited them to come away and pray with him. They had seen him pray many times, even prayed with him; they thought they knew what they were getting into, and then . . . *this!* Their eyes were opened to what happened in the spiritual realm when God the Son prayed. They saw Divine Light coursing through his humanity. They witnessed him listening to the Father as He addressed Jesus through Moses and Elijah, representing Israel's Law and prophets; and they heard Jesus respond in turn. And then within a matter of moments it was over, everything back to normal. Jesus stood before them alone, the same thirty-something man they had spent the past year with, wandering around Galilee and Judea. I wonder, though— did they brace themselves the next time Jesus began to pray? I know I would have; God the Son's prayer can be overwhelming, to say the least!

So imagine my shock when I read these words from Cardinal Joseph Ratzinger (later, Pope Benedict XVI): "Since the center of the person of Jesus is prayer, it is essential to participate in his prayer if we are to know and understand him."[1] The first part of his statement is easy enough to understand: Jesus is the Son of the Father. That is his deepest identity, from all of eternity. When he became a

---

1. Joseph Ratzinger, *Behold the Pierced One: An Approach to a Spiritual Christology* (Ignatius Press: San Francisco, 1986), 25.

xix

man he expressed his dependence on and love of the Father through communal and private prayer. He worshiped in the Temple and synagogue and communicated with the Father privately day and night. But how are we supposed to *participate*, take part, in his prayer? We're not there with him in the Temple or on the Mount of Transfiguration the way the Apostles were!

This is where our Catholic Faith comes to the rescue. It teaches that in baptism we were made members of a great mystical body of which Jesus is the head (1 Cor. 12:12–13; Eph. 4:15). Jesus is living his life within us, and so when we pray, "he prays in us, and with us."[2] To grow in intimacy with Jesus and share his prayer, his relationship with the Father, it is not necessary to travel back in time to the Transfiguration. The Church's liturgy and devotions can insert us, living right here and now, into Jesus's life of prayer. All we need to do is reach out and start using the rich treasury of prayer existing all around us as Catholics.

I know that is a bold claim. I could not have imagined making it twenty-six years ago, when I started my faith journey. I was a middle school student in a Catholic school who felt he "got nothing out of" going to Mass or reciting the prayers he had memorized for religion class, when an intense personal encounter with God—a transfiguration moment, you might say—turned my world upside down. I was hungry to know more of him and, because I had never encountered him through Catholic ritual or rote prayer, decided those were not of value. When a family friend invited me to her non-denominational (charismatic) church, I saw spontaneous, emotional prayer; and it seemed so much more authentic than the prayer I had grown up with. My mother and I started attending Tuesday night services, and I was well on my way to severing all ties with the Catholic Church if not for two things—an experience at Mass and then meeting a Catholic youth minister.

That Mass was nothing out of the ordinary; at least, it was not up until the point when I received Jesus in Communion. As I knelt in prayer I was absolutely overwhelmed by God's presence within me.

2. *Catechism of the Catholic Church* (*CCC*), 2nd ed. (Vatican City: Libreria Editrice Vaticana, 1997), 2740.

It was completely unexpected and personally undeniable. I was taken aback by the implication—Jesus gave himself to me through the ritual of the Mass. Perhaps there was more to those traditional Catholic prayers than I had thought.

Soon after that experience, my path crossed that of a dynamic Catholic youth minister who invited me to visit a newly formed prayer group for teens. The group brought all of the exuberance and prayerful spontaneity of the non-denominational church to its weekly meetings, but fused this with a monthly celebration of the Eucharist and retreats where we learned about the power of the sacrament of reconciliation, the Rosary, and praying the Liturgy of the Hours. We heard stories of the saints and the ways they prayed. I was able to look at the group's adult leaders and see the effects these traditional forms of prayer had on them and, in some cases, experienced them for myself.

The prayers of the Church and of her saints, rather than stifling my ability to express myself to God, enlarged it. I slowly came to see how the spontaneous, "authentic" prayers I offered at the beginning of my faith journey were those of a youngster—heartfelt and sincere but focused on my life and the small circle of lives touching mine. It was limited by my lack of knowledge regarding both the deepest needs and movements of the human heart and how prayer could be more than thought and words. The prayers of the Church are those of an adult with 2,000 years of spiritual depth and know-how. When I listened to her pray, especially at Mass, I was called out of myself, called to pray for and with the whole body of Christ—on earth, in purgatory, and in heaven! I was called to pray, fast, and do penance both for my sins and for my brothers' and sisters' sins. Left to myself I don't know how I ever could have arrived at the realization that all of our daily activities, even suffering, can be transformed into prayer!

Studying the gospels and the religious life of Jewish people in first-century Palestine convinces me that the Church did not arrive at the content or manner of her prayer lightly. I found the same concerns and practices in the prayer of Jesus himself! The Church's rich spiritual life is the work of the same Holy Spirit through which Jesus poured himself out in prayer to the Father.

In the pages that follow we will use Scripture and history to explore Jesus's prayer and recognize how Catholic liturgy, sacraments, devotions, and practices allow us not only to mirror his prayer, but to enter into it. We want to give ourselves to the Father, in the Holy Spirit, in union with Jesus. We will begin with his Incarnation and the prayers of his Jewish boyhood and move progressively forward to his Passion and the priesthood he now exercises in heaven. Chapters begin by exploring Jesus's prayer at a certain period in his life and then reflect upon which sacraments, elements of the Mass, and devotional practices make present those facets of Jesus's prayer. I then provide suggestions for how you can integrate these Catholic treasures into your spiritual life. The final chapters of the book are devoted to what I have come to view as the two greatest means, outside of the Eucharist, for bringing our prayer and lives into profound union with Jesus's—devotion to his Sacred Heart and Blessed Mother. I hope that reading this book will lead to a transfiguration moment in your own life, allowing you to see our centuries-old prayers and devotions for the spiritual livewires they are, and in doing so to be better equipped to fulfill the command to "[r]ejoice always; pray constantly; give thanks in all circumstances; for this is the will of God in Christ Jesus for you" (1 Thess. 5:16–18).

1

The Son's Prayer Enters Time

The mystery of the Most Holy Trinity is . . . the source of all the other mysteries of faith, the light that enlightens them. ⏤CCC 234

Christian prayer is . . . the action of God and of man, springing forth from both the Holy Spirit and ourselves, wholly directed to the Father, in union with the human will of the Son of God made man.
⏤CCC 2564

JESUS'S PRAYER LIFE began at conception, in the very act of becoming a child. It was not prayer as we normally conceive of it—thoughts expressed in words—but of an existence completely oriented toward and offered in love to the Father. That prayer became ours the moment we became Christians.

JESUS AT PRAYER

In the Womb

The writer of the Epistle to the Hebrews was allowed to "hear" Jesus's prayer as he entered the womb of Mary. "When Christ came into the world, he said, 'Sacrifices and [sin] offerings you have not desired, but a body you have prepared for me. . . . I have come to do your will, O God'" (Heb. 10:5–7; Ps. 40:6–8). Jesus's humanity, from the instant it came into being, was completely oriented toward the Father.

That first cry of his heart was the expression, in time and space, of the relationship he and the Father shared in eternity. As Son, he constantly receives the divine nature and all he is from the Father. Just as the Father pours himself out completely to the Son, so, too, the Son to the Father. Throughout eternity the two make a gift of themselves, communicate all that they are to each other in a perfect rush of love—the Holy Spirit.[1]

This relationship burst into our world in Jesus's conception. As an act of love offered by the Son to the Father, Jesus's conception was by the power of the Holy Spirit (Matt. 1:20; Luke 1:35). Jesus's whole humanity, body and soul, were united to the constant offering the Son makes of himself to the Father in the bosom of the Trinity. Beginning at the instant of his conception, and extending throughout his infancy, Jesus was engaged in a simple yet sublime form of prayer—that of "gazing" upon his Father in the heights of his soul and resting in His presence.[2]

Prayer, at its deepest level, is a matter not of words and gestures, but of the heart. Prayer flows from this hidden center—the place of decision, deeper than thought or emotion.[3] It is in his human heart that Jesus made his offering to the Father—not in words and gestures, but by *being*, by being a gestating child.

Introduction to the Prayer of His People

To Mary and Joseph belonged the privilege of helping Jesus acquire a "prayer language"—the words and gestures through which he could unite his mind and body to the prayer already taking place in his heart. They taught him the time-honored traditions of Jewish prayer.[4] They modeled, and then practiced with him, the words, devotional practices, and religious rites used by his ancestors to express their hearts to the Lord. They began the night of his birth.

---

1. We might refer to the Holy Spirit as the "prayer" within the Trinity.

2. John Saward, *Redeemer in the Womb* (San Francisco: Ignatius Press, 1993), 73, 137.

3. CCC 2562–63.

4. "The Son of God who became Son of the Virgin learned to pray in his human heart ... in the words and rhythms of his people, in the synagogue at Nazareth and the Temple at Jerusalem" (CCC 2599).

There in the cave of the nativity, his small ears heard Joseph intone the *Shema* before he and Mary drifted off to sleep. It was (and is) the creed prayed by faithful Jews at the beginning and end of each day: "Hear [*Shema* in Hebrew], O Israel! The LORD is our God, the LORD alone! Therefore, you shall love the LORD, your God, with all your heart, and with all your soul, and with all your strength. Take to heart these words which I enjoin on you today. Drill them into your children" (Deut. 6:4–7).[5] As an adult Jesus identified the *Shema* as the greatest of the Law of Moses's 613 commandments (Mark 12:29–30).

When he was eight days old, Joseph and Mary had Jesus circumcised. It was his first experience of the rites of Judaism. Given as the sign of God's covenant with Abraham, circumcision initiated Jesus into the Jewish community. It was also when he officially received his name (Luke 2:21).

Before we delve more deeply into Jesus's participation in the prayer life of Israel, however, let us stop and reflect upon how what we have seen in this chapter impacts our communal and individual prayer as Catholics. Think for a moment: The life of the Trinity, conception by the Holy Spirit, entrance into the community of faith—these are all brought together in baptism.

THE CHURCH AT PRAYER

The Sacrament of Baptism

Our first experience of the Christian life, the one that makes it possible for us to share Jesus's prayer, is our contact with the waters of baptism. Few sights are as familiar to a Catholic as that of a proud mother and father holding their child before a baptismal font. There, surrounded by godparents, family, and friends, their priest pours the baptismal waters over their child's head, saying, "I baptize you in the name of the Father, and of the Son, and of the Holy Spirit." It is probably so familiar to us, in fact, that it would be good

---

5. *New American Bible.*

to take a step back and renew our awe for the sacrament. Baptism gives us a share in Jesus's conception by the power of the Holy Spirit, transforming us from creatures of God into His sons and daughters; and that is the very foundation of our prayer.[6]

Unlike Jesus, each of us came into the world damaged. Genesis tells the story of our first parents' sin. Created as God's children (Gen. 1:26, 5:3), our first parents succumbed to the serpent's temptation to doubt God's goodness toward them. When they sinned they rejected God's fatherhood, forced the Holy Spirit from their souls, and damaged the human nature they passed onto us. Now, instead of souls docile to the Holy Spirit's movements, even the most innocent child comes into the world with a heart not naturally docile to the love of God. Sin changed the nature of prayer, too. It was no longer a child's expression of affection and dependence upon a heavenly Father, but a creature expressing homage and making petitions of a distant sovereign.

But the waters of baptism reverse that. As they wash over us, the Holy Spirit rushes into our souls and unites us to Jesus. We become sons and daughters *in the Son*. Our souls participate in Jesus's conception by the power of the Holy Spirit, and we are "born anew, not of perishable seed but of imperishable" (1 Pet. 1:23). We are even made "partakers of the divine nature" (2 Pet. 1:4).

Baptism empowers us to pray as God's children. "God has sent the Spirit of his Son into our hearts, crying, 'Abba! Father!'" (Gal. 4:6).[7] The Holy Spirit immediately sets about reproducing Jesus's prayer within the depths of our hearts. Like Jesus's prayer in the months between his conception and birth, it is prayer that transcends human language: "[T]he Spirit helps us in our weakness; for we do not know how to pray as we ought, but the Spirit himself intercedes for us with sighs too deep for words. And he who searches the hearts of men knows what is the mind of the Spirit, for

6. CCC 2565.

7. "Christian prayer is . . . the action of God and of man, springing forth from both the Holy Spirit and ourselves, wholly directed to the Father, in union with the human will of the Son of God made man." (CCC 2564)

the Spirit intercedes for the saints according to the will of God" (Rom. 8:26–27). When a child is baptized, do we realize what the Spirit is doing in their souls, how he is conforming their prayer to the wordless prayer of the infant Jesus?

Baptism also connects us to the rite of circumcision. Just as that rite, performed when Jesus was eight days old, brought him into God's covenant and the religious community of Israel, so baptism brings us—even as infants—into the New Covenant and makes us members of Christ's mystical body, the Church. Physical circumcision is no longer required because, as St. Paul taught, baptism cuts away the carnal, sinful desires from our hearts—the desires that have kept us from loving and obeying our heavenly Father (Col. 2:11–13; Rom. 2:26–29). It wipes away original sin and gives us the grace to overcome its effects. It is the fulfillment of Israel's prophecies: "Israel is uncircumcised in heart. . . . But this is the covenant which I will make with the house of Israel after those days, says the LORD: I will put my law within them, and I will write it upon their hearts" (Jer. 9:26, 31:33); "I will sprinkle clean water upon you, and you shall be clean. . . . I will take out of your flesh the heart of stone and give you a heart of flesh. I will put my spirit within you and cause you to walk in my statutes" (Ezek. 36:25–27).

The Creed and Sign of the Cross

Baptism is where we profess our faith in God. In a reversal of the original sin, we reject Satan and his empty promises and instead profess our faith in the Father, Son, and Spirit. We do this by expressing our agreement with the Apostles' Creed. If we were brought to the sacrament as infants, then our parents expressed agreement in our names—reflections of Mary and Joseph praying the *Shema* as they knelt beside Christ's manger. And often the first prayer Christian parents teach their children is the Sign of the Cross, the Creed in miniature.

The Sign of the Cross is so familiar to us that we often forget the magnitude of what we profess when we make it. Recall the words of the *Shema*: "The LORD is our God, the LORD alone! Therefore, you shall love the LORD, your God, with all your heart, and with all your soul [or mind], and with all your strength." Now slowly make the Sign of the Cross: "In the Name of the Father (touch your forehead), and of the Son (touch your heart), and of the Holy Spirit (touch both shoulders)." In that simple blessing we proclaimed the Gospel, the Good News, of Jesus Christ: Through his Cross we enter into the inner life of the Father, Son, and Holy Spirit—and by his grace we have been empowered to fulfill the greatest commandment, with all our mind, all our heart, and all our strength. That is the power of the Sign of the Cross! That is the reason we use it to begin and end each of our times of prayer.

Holy Images and Eucharistic Adoration

The prayer of the infant Jesus—his silent repose in the presence of the Father—and the ability to participate in his prayer that was given to us at baptism means that we Christians can pray even when grief, confusion, and exhaustion leave us at a total loss for words. Jesus's Incarnation gives us concrete helps that, even in our darkest moments, allow us to place our hearts in God's presence: our use of images and the ability to visit Jesus in the Eucharist.

When God the Son became a man, it finally became possible for us to visualize God. He has a *human face* that can be represented to us in art.[8] When we find ourselves overwhelmed and at a loss for what to say to God, we can look to the images of Jesus in our homes—the crucifix, a favorite icon or painting, a holy card—and let them speak the message for which they were crafted: "I am with you always" (Matt. 28:20).

We can allow our eyes to rest on that image a few moments as we drink in the truth that Jesus dwells in our souls. We can slowly make the Sign of the Cross and intentionally place ourselves in God's presence, trusting the Holy Spirit given to us in baptism to intercede on our behalf "with sighs too deep for words" (Rom. 8:26).

The second way—the fullest way—to place ourselves in God's presence is to visit Jesus in the Eucharist, either in the tabernacle of

---

8. CCC 1159–60.

the church or exposed in the monstrance of the adoration chapel.[9] Catholics believe that out of love for us, not only did the Son of God become a helpless child, he abased himself even further by taking on the appearance of bread and giving himself to us as food! It was no accident that the only "bed" Mary and Joseph could find to lay Jesus in that first night was a manger, a feed box for animals. It was divine foreshadowing of the night thirty-three years later when he blessed and broke the bread, saying, "This is my body" (Matt. 26:26).

Whenever we enter the sanctuary of a church or an adoration chapel, we physically, objectively, place ourselves in the presence of God. Whether we are aware of it or not, despite whatever our emotions might be telling us, or how distracted our minds may be, by the very act of coming before him, we have begun to pray.

If we are in an adoration chapel, then we can fix our eyes on Jesus exposed for us in the monstrance. We can gaze on him *as he gazes upon the Father in heaven*. We sit or kneel in his presence and allow the Holy Spirit to cry out from the depths of our souls, "Abba! Father!" and lift up to God all the things we are unable to articulate.

9. The adoration chapel is where the Eucharist is reserved in a monstrance. The Host, Jesus, is visible to our eyes there upon the altar. Some Catholic parishes have adoration chapels open to the public twenty-four hours a day. Others are open for several hours a day. To find the one closest to your home, please contact your local diocese by phone or the web.

2

A Pilgrim to the Temple

Jesus venerated the Temple by going up to it for the Jewish feasts of pilgrimage, and with a jealous love he loved this dwelling of God among men. The Temple prefigures his own mystery. ⌇CCC 593

A better knowledge of the Jewish people's faith and religious life as professed and lived even now can help our better understanding of certain aspects of Christian liturgy. ⌇CCC 1096

✝

IT WOULD BE near impossible to overstate the centrality of the Temple in the life of a first-century Jew. The Holy Family, like the vast majority of families living in Palestine, made regular pilgrimage there to take part in its rituals. Here in America today, with our strong emphasis on the individual, it has become difficult to see the value in ritual, or liturgy; unless our actions and prayer are spontaneous, we have difficulty believing that they flow from the heart. But this mindset could not be further from the thought of Jesus, Mary, and Joseph. The Jerusalem Temple—with its priesthood, sacrifices, and daily liturgy—was the foundation upon which the spiritual life of the synagogue *and the individual* were built. Not only did Luke the Evangelist begin and end his Gospel there, the only two events he narrates from Jesus's childhood occurred there.[1]

In this chapter we will deepen our understanding of the worship Jesus engaged in at the Temple. We will clarify the meaning of sacrifice for the Jewish people and the function of the priesthood, as well

---

1. Jesus's presentation in the Temple (Luke 2:22–39) and finding in the Temple at age twelve (Luke 2:41–51).

8

as increase our knowledge of the Temple's system of courts, and the rules concerning who could proceed deeper into its interior. Then in the second half of the chapter, we will discover how Jesus's worship in the earthly Temple is brought to completion in the worship we offer the Father—through, with, and in Jesus—at Mass.

JESUS AT PRAYER

The Inestimable Value of the Temple

The Jewish people knew that the Creator of the universe could not be contained in a building made of stone (1 Kings 8:27). No one knew this better than the God-Man, and yet Jesus reverenced the Temple as "my Father's house" (Luke 2:49; John 2:16). The Temple was heaven's embassy on earth, *the place* where the utterly transcendent God came to meet His people. It was patterned after the Tabernacle, the portable sanctuary Moses constructed in the desert in response to a pattern God had shown him (Exod. 25:9, 40). Its heart, its innermost chamber, was the Holy of Holies; for hundreds of years it was the resting place of the Ark of the Covenant, above which God was said to sit "enthroned" (Ps. 80:1, 99:1; 2 Kings 19:15). Like Moses before the burning bush, Jerusalem's Temple was *adamat-qodesh*, holy ground.

It was the place where God commanded His people to come in pilgrimage to worship. And the worship He commanded was very specific—*avodah*, sacrifice (Deut. 12:13–14). It is understandable that we today, living in a largely urban society, are mystified as to why God would ask for animal sacrifices. The Israelites were people of the land, though; they either raised their own food or lived just down a dirt path from the people they purchased it from. Ultimately, sacrifice was not about spilling blood. When God asked them to sacrifice animals from their flocks, or a portion of their produce, bread, and wine, He was asking them, in a very literal way, to share their *lives* with Him (Lev. 17:11, 23:18; Exod. 29:38–42). In hindsight we recognize that God was revealing what it means to be His sons and daughters—to image the Son in offering back to the

9

Father all that we have received. Under the Old Covenant, however, it occurred in a veiled way.

Although sacrifice was the foundation of the Israelites' spiritual lives, a rich tapestry of songs, verbal prayers, and actions grew up around it in the course of centuries. Before we study the liturgy experienced by Jesus, some background information is in order.

Background—Levitical Priesthood, Laity, and Pilgrimage

It is one of the great ironies that when Jesus, the High Priest of the New Covenant, visited the Temple he did so *as a layman*. Even though all of Israel was "a kingdom of priests" (Exod. 19:6), only males from the tribe of Levi, one of the twelve tribes that formed Israel, were called by God to serve in the Temple. Jesus was born into the same tribe as King David, the tribe of Judah, and was therefore ineligible for any type of liturgical ministry. When Joseph and Mary presented Jesus in the Temple forty days after his birth, they were "redeeming" him from priestly service—paying five shekels to the Levites who would serve God liturgically in Jesus's place (Num. 18:15–16).

All Levites were eligible to fill roles of service within the Temple, but only descendants of Moses's brother Aaron were eligible to serve as priests. Only they offered the people's gifts upon the great altar. And of them, only the high priest entered the Holy of Holies—on one day of the year, *Yom Kippur*, the Day of Atonement.

Devout Jews from all over the Roman world benefitted from the work of the Levites when they streamed toward Jerusalem for *Shalah Regilam*, the Three Pilgrimages. The Law of Moses required Israelites to come to the Temple for the feast of Passover in the spring, Pentecost fifty days later, and the feast of Tabernacles in the fall (Exod. 23:14–17, 34:22–23). Luke's Gospel refers to this when it says the Holy Family "went to Jerusalem every year at the feast of the Passover" (Luke 2:41). The three feasts celebrated the past (deliverance in the Passover, the giving of the Law at Pentecost, and the entrance into the Promised Land at Tabernacles) while looking ahead to a new fulfillment when the Messiah arrived—unequaled freedom, faithfulness, and prosperity. John's Gospel shows Jesus traveling back and forth between Galilee and Jerusalem to celebrate the great feasts. He even made the trip for a non-required feast such as *Hanukkah* (John 10:22–24). No matter which feast Jesus attended, and despite the special elements attached to each one, Jesus would always have seen the same daily liturgy being carried out by the Levites—and for the simple reason that the Lord had commanded it.

Attending the Daily Liturgy

Singing the Songs of Ascents (Psalms 120–134) along with his fellow pilgrims, Jesus's heart probably quickened when Jerusalem came into view. There, perched on Mt. Moriah, he would have seen his Father's house. Josephus, a Jewish historian writing at the end of the first century, described it thus:

> The outward face of the temple ... was covered all over with plates of gold of great weight, and, at the first rising of the sun, [it] reflected back a fiery splendor, and made those who forced themselves to look upon it to turn their eyes away, just as they would have done at the sun's own rays. (*The Wars of the Jews* 5.5.222)[2]

Jesus would have entered the first of the Temple's four courts, that of the Gentiles. It was populated by money changers and merchants selling animals for the pilgrims' sacrifices.[3] It was the only area into which non-Jews were welcome. A large sign announced that any Gentile who went farther "will have himself to blame for his death which will follow."

The next court Jesus and his fellow Jews entered, carrying their sacrificial gifts, was the court of the women. This was as far as his mother was allowed to accompany him. The Temple treasury was there. All males over the age of twenty contributed to the upkeep of the Temple, a half shekel yearly (Exod. 30:11–16). At the end of the court were the fifteen semi-circular steps that climbed to the court of the men. On a great feast like that of Tabernacles, a choir made up of

2. William Whiston, *Josephus: The Complete Works* (Dallas: Thomas Nelson, 1998), 848.
3. Much of the coinage used at the time bore images and inscriptions religiously offensive to Jews. To purchase sacrificial animals at the Temple, pagan coinage had to be exchanged for the "shekel of the Sanctuary," with money changers taking a profit.

Levites stood on the steps and sang the Songs of Ascents as pious men, *hassidim*, swung torches and danced through the women's courtyard.

The court of the Israelites, the court of the men, was only nineteen feet wide. From here Jesus could see into the court of the priests where the lives of the animals were taken and part of their bodies burned on the enormous altar. (The altar was so large that priests had to climb a ramp to reach the top.)

If Jesus gazed into the court of the priests at either nine o'clock in the morning or three o'clock in the afternoon, then he would have seen the priests setting up for the *tamid*, the daily offering of a lamb, cake of bread, and wine (Exod. 29:38–41). He watched one set of priests, clad in white linen, purify their hands and feet in the "bronze sea," a large basin, as another set blessed the Lord and led the people in the recitation of the Ten Commandments and the *Shema*.

As we saw in the first chapter, the *Shema* was Judaism's chief creed. Most of us are only familiar with its beginning; it is actually quite lengthy, composed of three separate passages of Scripture (which due to space constraints I can only quote a portion of):

> Hear, O Israel: The LORD our God is one LORD; and you shall love the LORD your God with all your heart, and with all your soul, and with all your might. And these words which I command you this day shall be upon your heart; and you shall teach them diligently to your children. . . . (Deut. 6:4–9)

> And if you will obey my commandments . . . he will give the rain for your land in its season . . . and you shall eat and be full. Take heed lest your heart be deceived, and you turn aside and serve other gods and worship them, and the anger of the LORD be kindled against you, and he will shut up the heavens. . . . (Deut. 11:13–21)

> The LORD said to Moses, "Speak to the sons of Israel, and bid them to make tassels on the corners of their garments . . . and it shall be to you a tassel to look upon and remember all the commandments of the LORD, to do them, not follow after your own heart and your own eyes. . . ." (Num. 15:37–41)[4]

---

4. Here the three portions of the *Shema* have been abbreviated; the reader is highly encouraged to read them in their entirety.

The *Shema* was immediately followed by the *tamid*. As the priests placed a lamb, cake of bread, and wine on the altar, trumpets sounded and everyone in the Temple prostrated themselves on the ground.

When Jesus rose, he saw Levites gathering above him on the wall dividing the Court of the Men from that of the Priests. They led the worshipers in singing the *Tehillim*, the Psalms. In Jesus's time the Psalms were not a book of poems, but hymns; and each weekday had been assigned its own. Worshipers throughout the Temple were alerted to its beginning by a crash of cymbals. Here is a sampling:

Sunday—Psalm 24

Who shall ascend the hill of the LORD?/And who shall stand in his holy place?/He who has clean hands and a pure heart. . . . (v. 3)

Monday—Psalm 48

We have thought on your mercy, O God,/in the midst of your temple.
As your name, O God, so your praise, reaches to the ends of the earth. . . . (vv. 9–10)

Tuesday—Psalm 82

Arise, O God, judge the earth;/for to you belong all the nations! (v. 8)

Wednesday—Psalm 94

Blessed is the man whom you chasten, O LORD, /and whom you teach out of your law. (v. 12)

Thursday—Psalm 81

Sing aloud to God our strength…/Raise a song, sound the timbrel, the sweet lyre with the harp. . . . (vv. 1–2)

Friday—Psalm 93

The LORD reigns; he is robed in majesty; /the Lord is robed, he is girded with strength. (v. 1)

Saturday, the Sabbath—Psalm 92

It is good to give thanks to the LORD, /to sing praises to your name, O Most High/[The righteous] are planted in the house of the LORD, /they flourish in the courts of our God. (vv. 1, 13)

13

As the Levites paused between each section in the psalm, the trumpets sounded and everyone prostrated themselves.

What Jesus or anyone outside of the priesthood never saw was the part of the daily offering that took place within the *Hekal*, the Holy Place, or ante-chamber to the Holy of Holies. After a priest ascended the staircase from the court of the priests, he stepped into a room overlaid in pure gold, illuminated by the menorah, the seven-branched lampstand. At the far end of the room hung the thick curtain cordoning off the Holy of Holies. The priest passed a table holding twelve loaves of bread, one for each tribe of Israel. (It was known as the bread of the Presence, literally "bread of the Face," and was considered a symbol of the coming Messiah.)[5] The priest finally came to a small altar where he burned incense before the Holy of Holies.[6] For him to have proceeded any further would have elicited the death sentence. Only the high priest could do so, once a year on the Day of Atonement, when he entered after sprinkling the blood of a bull and goat on the curtain before him.[7]

If it was the three o'clock offering, then the daily liturgy concluded with the priests gathering on the steps to the *Hekal* and blessing the people with the blessing God entrusted to their first high priest, Aaron: "The LORD [YHWH] bless you and keep you; The LORD [YHWH] make his face to shine upon you, and be gracious to you: the LORD lift up his countenance upon you, and give you peace" (Num. 6:24–26). When the name YHWH was spoken aloud, all in the Temple went down on their knees, faces in their hands, responding, "Blessed be the Name of His glorious kingdom forever." And so ended the daily liturgy.

Between the morning and afternoon liturgies the priests were in constant motion, offering pilgrims' individual sacrifices upon the altar. The man on Jesus's right may have carried unleavened bread

5. Michael Keenan Jones, *Toward A Theology Of Christ the High Priest* (Rome: Editrice Pontifica Universita Gregoriana, 2006), 38.

6. John the Baptist's father Zechariah was doing this when the Archangel Gabriel appeared to him (Luke 1:8–11).

7. Once inside the Holy of Holies, he sprinkled the blood in the Lord's presence, symbolically offering the Lord back the gift of life that he had bestowed, thereby obtaining pardon for the nation's sins committed in the past year.

and wine, the blessings of the harvest. The man on Jesus's left might have sought God's forgiveness as well as help for his family. The father behind Jesus may have come to offer a bull in thanks to God for saving him from disease; his sacrifice was called a *todah* (thank) offering. In many offerings, the *todah* being an example, a portion of the animal was offered on the altar, a part held back to be eaten by the priests, and a part eaten by the family making the offering. In this way God and His people were united in the life of the sacrificial victim; communion was established, or re-established after a lapse into sin. Communion made the laity "partners in the altar" (1 Cor. 10:18).

Something Greater Than the Temple

"That's very impressive," you might think, "but how exactly does this apply to us twenty-first-century Christians? As close as the Temple and the liturgy brought God to people, He always remained just out of reach—just beyond that court, or just beyond that curtain." And the answer is that the Temple was never meant as an end in itself; it always pointed to a greater reality—Jesus's offering on the Cross and the access we all have to God in the liturgy of the Mass. King Solomon modeled his Temple on a vision seen by Moses (Exod. 25:40; 1 Chron. 28:19).[8] Four hundred years later, however, Ezekiel the prophet received a vision of the ideal Temple, one far grander than Solomon's (Ezek. 40:1–47:12). The Temple Ezekiel saw had a river flowing out of it, a river so powerful it put the desert into a perpetual state of bloom (Ezek. 47:1–12); and Jesus, the God-Man, is that new Temple, and the Holy Spirit that gushes from his human heart to ours the river.

Jesus taught that he did not come to abolish but to fulfill the Law and the Prophets and the Temple of which they spoke. John's Gospel drives this truth home when John tells us that Jesus's words about how "the Temple" would be destroyed and rebuilt in three days referred not to the sanctuary, but to his *physical body* (2:19–22).

---

8. The Temple had to be rebuilt following its destruction by the Babylonians in 586 BC. The Temple Jesus worshiped in, following the same pattern as Solomon's, was the beneficiary of an enrichment and enlargement program funded by King Herod.

John's Gospel also tells us how Jesus stood up at the feast of Tabernacles, with its water drawing ceremony, and called everyone who was thirsty to drink from *the river of living water that would flow from his heart*; John explains that "this he said about the Spirit, which those who believed in him were to receive; for as yet the Spirit had not been given, because Jesus was not yet glorified" (John 7:39). The Gospel then shows us the moment when the Spirit began to flow from the new Temple, Jesus, to the believer: when the Roman soldier pierced Jesus's side with a spear, and blood *and water* flowed out (John 19:34).

Jesus's death, the piercing of his heart, opened our way to the Father. The synoptic gospels teach the same truth when they tell us how Jesus's death caused the curtain sealing off the Holy of Holies to be ripped in two, "from top to bottom" (Matt. 27:51; Mark 15:38; Luke 23:45). God had finally overcome all the boundaries our sin had set up to living in union with Him and with one another, the very boundaries represented by the Temple's courts and curtain!

Jesus was the human being who finally made a complete and perfect return of himself to the Father, from the first instant of his conception all the way to his last breath on the Cross . . . and even beyond death through his resurrection and ascension. The sacrificial animals offered to God in smoke from the Temple's altar found their reality in Jesus's passage to the Father; and just as the laity and priests participated in the sacrifice by eating a portion of it, so we participate in Jesus's offering by receiving him in Eucharistic Communion.

THE CHURCH AT PRAYER

Sacrifice, the symbolic pouring out of our lives to God, was the foundation of Israel's worship, its prayer; and the same is true of us. Jesus's offering and the Church's obedience to his command to "Do *this*," and to re-present his sacrifice in the Eucharist, is the source and summit of our Faith. (CCC 1324) At Mass, the elements of Jesus's worship in the Temple—holy ground and the Holy of Holies, pilgrimage, sacrifice and priesthood, the Psalms and *Shema*, Communion and blessing—are transformed, and we participate in them today.

Our Tabernacle and Sanctuary

Any time we enter a Catholic sanctuary, we genuflect before the tabernacle. We do so because we know Jesus is present there as he is in no other place in the world—body, blood, soul, and divinity. That tabernacle, that small golden box, is a modern-day Holy of Holies.[9] It's even more than that. The Temple's Holy of Holies was an earthly throne room where the Creator was somehow mysteriously present and accessible; but in the tabernacle, because of the Incarnation and the words of consecration, our Creator is personally and *substantially* present.

The holiness of his presence extends outward from the tabernacle to claim the entire sanctuary. It is holy ground. We quiet our voices whenever we enter, instinctively realizing that we have entered God's presence in a new way. Up those steps, on the altar, is where Jesus's sacrifice becomes present.[10]

This sanctuary is different from the one in Jerusalem, though; there are no walls of separation. Jew and Gentile, man and woman—all worship together. The Church and its sanctuary are *catholic*, universal. Baptism has made us "all one in Christ Jesus" (Gal. 3:28). The holiness of Christ and his Church is meant to extend beyond the sanctuary into the midst of the world. Because Jesus is the Temple, we his mystical body are as well—both corporately and individually; and as we use the Spirit's gifts in service to one another, the Temple grows (Eph. 2:21–22).

---

9. It is also one of the realities prefigured by the Bread of the Presence, the "bread of the Face," kept in the *Hekal.*

10. There are of course a number of Christians who do not share the Catholic understanding of "sacred space." They misunderstand Jesus's words to the Samaritan woman: "the hour is coming when neither on this mountain nor in Jerusalem will you worship the Father. . . . But the hour is coming, and now is, when the true worshipers will worship the Father in spirit and truth. . . . God is spirit, and those who worship him must worship in spirit and truth" (John 4:21–24). It is not that holy ground has ceased to exist, but that the possibility of finding it has increased exponentially—it exists wherever the Blessed Sacrament is present for worship by the baptized, those born of the Spirit and truth.

The Sunday Obligation and Liturgical Calendar

Jesus made pilgrimages to the Father's House, and so do we. Each Sunday that we fulfill our obligation to attend Mass, our walk or drive to the sanctuary is a miniature pilgrimage. We even have holy days of obligation that, like the Three Pilgrimages in Judaism, require us to celebrate Mass during the week. As a Jew, Jesus celebrated a number of other feasts throughout the year; and as Catholics we have a liturgical calendar populated with not just mysteries from the lives of Jesus and Mary, but a cadre of canonized brothers and sisters in whom we celebrate the victory of God's grace every day of the year. Our Faith is so dense, and the witness of the saints so extraordinary, that it has to be spread out this way so that we can focus our gaze upon one or two elements at a time; otherwise God's grace is simply too mind-boggling!

The Priesthood

For Christians there is really only one priest, Jesus. (CCC 1545) However, just as baptism makes us to share in Jesus's Sonship and identity as God's Temple, so it also makes us share his priesthood (1 Pet. 2:9). We offer our whole lives—our public and private prayer being a facet—to the Father, through the Spirit, in union with Jesus. When one of the laity is ordained to the ministerial priesthood, he begins to participate in Jesus's priesthood in a different way. Unlike the levitical priests, he is not a "go-between" for us and God. Nor is he an obstacle placed between Christ and the laity. Our ordained priests are servants charged with *assisting us* to live out our identity. Our priests act *through, with, and in Jesus* to bring this about: leading us in the celebration of the Eucharist, hearing our confessions, speaking hard truths out of love, and interceding for our needs. Far from being an obstacle to union with Christ, our priests can bring Jesus and his saving mission directly, "physically," to us.

The Psalms and Creed

Every Mass, just like every liturgy in the Temple, makes use of the Psalms to praise and petition God. In most Masses we use the psalms as they were intended, not as poems but as songs. We can speak and sing to God in our own words, but when we pray the Psalms we pour our hearts out in words inspired by the Holy Spirit, the same words Jesus prayed when he was on earth!

Besides the Psalms, the daily liturgy in the Temple also included Judaism's Creed, the *Shema*: "Hear, O Israel: The LORD our God is one LORD...." Our Creed at Mass, the Niceno-Constantinopolitan Creed, illuminates the *Shema*'s witness to God's oneness with the revelation of Father, Son, and Spirit and salvation in Christ.

Our Creed should not just be recited—it should be *prayed*. Our voices should be filled with conviction and awe when we say, "On the third day *he rose again* in fulfillment of the Scriptures!... He will *come again in glory* to judge the living and the dead, *and his kingdom will have no end!*" We are proclaiming the truth about our Beloved for all of heaven and earth to hear. It should come from our depths, from our hearts, not solely from a list kept before the mind's eye or read from a missal.

The Church's Sacrifice

The Church cannot offer the Father a greater gift than His Son. The Eucharist was prefigured in the Temple's *tamid*—the daily offering of a lamb, bread, and wine. In the Eucharist, however, our gifts of bread and wine are transformed *into* the Lamb. Time and space are folded, and Jesus's sacrifice becomes present on that altar; we unite ourselves to him, putting all of our interior and exterior resources at his disposal (Rom. 12:1). Jesus catches us up, inserts us into himself, as he pours himself out, whole and entire, in the power of the Holy Spirit, to the Father.

Communion and Blessing

Eucharistic Communion is the absolute pinnacle of our spiritual lives, a taste of the endless union with the Trinity that we are journeying toward. It is not something that we have to "psyche ourselves up" for; it is an objective reality. The same Jesus who is glorified at the right hand of the Father *enters into you and me*. In what looks like common food and drink, we consume the one in whom "the fullness of deity dwells bodily" (Col. 2:9). We receive his flesh and blood into us. We receive his soul, his human heart, on fire with the Holy Spirit and poured out to the Father!

And then we are sent forth into the world, to make Jesus physically and verbally present to our family and colleagues. Through our presence and example, Jesus intends to draw the world to himself, to the Eucharist; he reminds them, as he did Mary and Joseph as a boy, that they can always find him in his Father's house (Luke 2:49). Like the levitical priests, our ordained priests send us forth by blessing us in the Name of the one Lord—Father, Son, and Holy Spirit. We walk out of Mass having just shared in the sacrifice of Jesus; every other prayer we offer, every other action we perform, now flows from this. As we say at the end of Mass, "Thanks be to God!"

3

In the Home and Synagogue

The Son of God . . . learned to pray in his human heart. He learns to pray from his mother, who kept all the great things the Almighty had done and treasured them in her heart. He learns to pray in the words and rhythms of the prayer of his people, in the synagogue at Nazareth. ⌐CCC 2599

For both Jews and Christians Sacred Scripture is an essential part of their respective liturgies. . . . In its characteristic structure the Liturgy of the Word originates in Jewish prayer. The Liturgy of the Hours and . . . the Lord's Prayer, have parallels in Jewish prayer.
⌐CCC 1096

HAVE YOU EVER had one of those "mountaintop" experiences, where you wonder how you will ever be able to prolong it once you go back down into the "valley" of everyday life? It might have been the intimacy you experienced with a spouse on a weekend away, or the complete absence of stress you felt while on a road trip with friends. It may have been an intense experience of God while on a retreat. I imagine that a Jewish person's visits to the Temple were "mountaintop" experiences, too. So how did you fare in bringing a piece of the mountain back down to earth with you? Did it survive the demands of your job, social calendar, and bills that needed paying? We could all learn quite a bit from the Jews.

They had an ingeniously intricate system of maintaining their spiritual lives between their hikes up Mt. Zion to the Temple. In this chapter we are going to examine the way Jesus and other first-century Jews wove prayer throughout the course of the day and came together as a community to study and pray in the synagogue. By doing this they were able to join all of their day-to-day activities and responsibilities to the blessing, thanking, and petitioning of God occurring in the Temple's liturgy. We will then explore how we Christians use these same avenues to join our daily activities to Jesus's eucharistic offering.

JESUS AT PRAYER

Sanctification of Everyday Activities

"Impressive" is the word that jumps to mind whenever I think of the amount of praying that occurred in a run-of-the-mill Jewish day. It started with the very act of waking and continued even as they settled into bed at night. It was not just the amount of prayer that I find so impressive, though—it was the disposition of the heart.

For someone like me, whose personal prayer seems fixated on asking God for help, the Jewish focus on blessing God—expressing awe, praise, and gratitude—stands out. *Berakah*, or blessing, was always at the forefront of the Jewish mind. Petition was there, too, but is always secondary to the movement of love. *Berakah* was the first thing that sprang from Mary's lips in the *Magnificat*: "My soul magnifies the Lord" (Luke 1:46) and Zechariah's in the *Benedictus*: "Blessed be the Lord God of Israel" (Luke 1:68).

Like all Jewish parents, Joseph and Mary would have taught Jesus how each morning provided a wealth of opportunities to bless the Lord. As soon as his eyes opened, he blessed God for removing "the bands of sleep" from his eyes. He would have blessed the Father for raising those who were stooped as he got up from his sleeping mat, as well as for the proper functioning of his body when he used the restroom. Everything was recognized for what it was—a gift from God's generous hands. Slipping on his robe was occasion for praising the way God clothes the naked.

Even the garments Jesus wore spoke of God. *Tzitzit*, linen fringes with a cord of blue, were sown to the edges of his clothing. When he recited the *Shema* each morning and evening, its third part spoke of the *tzitzit*'s significance: "to look upon and remember all the commandments of the LORD, to do them, not to follow after your own heart and your own eyes" (Num. 15:39).[1] Some modern biblical scholars see a connection between *tzitzit* and the garments of the levitical priests and hangings in the sanctuary; if correct, then the *tzitzit* were a direct and constant link to the life of the Temple.

Meals in the Jewish home were intimate affairs, an ongoing experience of God's generous provision. Taking bread, Joseph or Jesus prayed words still prayed in Jewish homes today: "Blessed are you, O Lord our God, King of the universe, who have brought forth bread from the earth."[2] (This was probably the blessing our Lord prayed later in life, before multiplying the loaves and fishes.) Some families offered blessings for each course in the meal. At the meal's conclusion, the *Birkat Hamazon* was offered—three benedictions, considered the oldest in Judaism.[3] God was blessed first for His provision of food, then for the Promised Land, and finally for Jerusalem, wherein lay the Temple. Whatever the activity, the Jewish people found a way to unite it to their identity as a priestly people (Exod. 19:6).

---

1. We hear of the *tzizit* in the gospels, in the stories of the woman with a hemorrhage (Matt. 9:20–21) and the sick of Gennesaret, who "begged [Jesus] that they might only touch the fringe of his garment; and as many as touched it were made well" (Matt. 14:36). It was also very common to wear *tefilin*, or phylacteries, during morning prayer. These were leather straps worn around the head and left arm, containing four verses from the Torah, all which mirrored the first: "It shall be to you as a sign on your hand and as a memorial between your eyes, that the law of the LORD may be in your mouth" (Exod. 13:9; see also Exod. 13:16 and Deut. 6:8). Some pious persons made a show by wearing extra wide phylacteries or continuing to wear them the entire day. Our Lord did not take kindly to that, not when done to attract attention to self, rather than to orient self to God (Matt. 23:1–12).

2. Steven B. Clark, *Introduction to the Eucharist* (Ann Arbor, MI: Servant Publications, 2000), 113.

3. Carmine DiSante, *Jewish Prayer: The Origins of the Christian Liturgy* (Mahwah, NJ: Paulist Press, 1991), 145. The *Birkat Hamazon* was offered in response to Deuteronomy 8:10: "And you shall eat and be full, and you shall bless the LORD your God for the good land he has given you."

Three Special Times of Prayer

In the previous chapter, we looked at the daily offering in the Temple, which took place at 9 AM and 3 PM. What I did not share at that point was how Jews at the time of Jesus, no matter where they lived, stopped at those times, turned toward Jerusalem, and united themselves to the liturgy of the Temple. They did so a third time around sunset, when the final scraps were burned on the altar and the Temple's gates closed. These three times of prayer are attested to as far back as 164 BC, when the book of Daniel reached its final form.[4]

During the morning and evening prayer, the *Shema* was recited —the spiritual bookends of the day. In the morning it was preceded by two benedictions: one blessing God for His creation of light and the other for His giving of the Law (Torah). The morning *Shema* was followed by a benediction blessing God for His faithfulness, especially that shown when He liberated Israel from Egypt. Prior to the evening *Shema*, God is blessed for the creation of night and the gift of the Torah that reveals life's meaning. The *Shema* is followed by a blessing of God for His faithfulness and a petition that He watch over those who sleep.

At all three times of prayer—morning, afternoon, and evening— Jews also prayed the Eighteen Benedictions. In Hebrew they are known as the *Tephilla*, simply "the prayer," a witness to their central place in Jewish life.[5] These eighteen blessings and petitions were the daily prayers of Joseph, Mary, Peter, and Paul—everyone we read about in the New Testament—but most importantly, Jesus himself. In Jesus's time, the theme of each benediction had been established, but the exact wording was left to the one praying. (It wasn't until after the fall of the Temple in AD 70, in an attempt to safeguard their heritage, that the rabbis insisted upon a fixed

---

4. Dan. 6:10, 13; see discussion in Joachim Jeremias, *The Prayers of Jesus* (Naperville, IL: Alec R. Allenson, Inc., 1967), 69.

5. Because the Eighteen Benedictions were always prayed while standing, it is also common to hear them referred to as the *Amidah*, from the Hebrew for "stand up." Jesus made reference to this: "And whenever you *stand praying*, forgive" (Mark 11:25).

wording for each.) In their simplest form, the benedictions would have been as follows:[6]

Blessed be the Lord. . . .

1) ...the God of Abraham, Isaac, and Jacob, our shield through the ages.

2) ...who raises the dead.

3) ...the only God.

4) ...who gives knowledge. Give us understanding of Your Law.

5) ...who loves repentance. Make us turn back to You.

6) ...who forgives. Forgive us our sins against You.

7) ...who has redeemed Israel. Save us from our enemies.

8) ...who heals the sick. Heal the pain in our hearts.

9) ...who blesses the yearly harvest. Send our lands all they need to be fruitful.

10) ...who gathers the exiles of Israel. Bring them back.

11) ...who loves justice. Give us wise judges and leaders, as we had in times past.

12) ...who humbles the arrogant, the heretics. Remove them from among Your people.[7]

---

6. I formulated this simplified rendering of the Eighteen Benedictions after studying their content in the following works: DiSante, *Jewish* Prayer, 89–106; Frederick C. Grant, *Ancient Judaism and The New Testament,* (New York: The Macmillan Co., 1959), 45–47; Joseph Heinemann and Jakob J. Petuchowski, eds., *Literature of the Synagogue* (New York: Behrman House, 1975), 34–36; Frederic Manns, *Jewish Prayer in the Time of Jesus* (Jerusalem: Franciscan Printing Press, 1994), 136–37.

7. We may be taken aback to think of Jesus, Mary, and Joseph praying such a benediction. The benedictions surrounding this one ask God to bring about the End Times, to come as Judge and put all things right; and one effect of God's coming as Judge will be to deal with those who have committed themselves to falsehood and encouraged others to do so. We Christians pray for the same thing, albeit implicitly, in the *Our Father*: "Thy kingdom come, Thy will be done, on earth as it is in heaven." Perhaps that was our Lord's way of positively recasting this benediction. As a historical note: When the language of the Eighteen Benedictions was fixed after the fall of the Temple in AD 70, Christians were identified as the heretics that God was asked to judge.

13) ...who shelters the righteous. Shower goodness upon converts and reward all who do Your will.

14) ...who rebuilt Jerusalem. Restore the kingdom of David, Your anointed one.

15) ...who hears our prayers.

16) ...who allows us to worship in His sanctuary. May He always dwell in Jerusalem.

17) ...whom it is right to thank. Thank You for the mercy, kindness, and goodness You have shown to us, and our fathers and mothers before us.

18) ...who creates peace. Give Your peace to Your people Israel.

I want you to look closely at the Eighteen Benedictions through Christian eyes. Look at what they ask of God; and now, consider: Every petition was answered, every blessing taken to a new level of reality, through Jesus's life, death, resurrection, and ascension! Jesus entered history at precisely the right moment, what Scripture calls the "fullness of time" (Gal. 4:4).[8] He came when these blessings and petitions would be a part of his prayer three times a day. This gets at a deep reality about prayer—that our prayers never "change God's mind." Rather, they have been *willed* from all of eternity. As God's partners, He has willed to release certain graces only in response to our prayers—and this most profoundly true with regard to Jesus's prayers. I suggest that when God willed the Incarnation, He simultaneously willed the petitions Jesus offered as a man, simultaneously willed to bring about Jesus's resurrection and all that would mean for humanity in response to them.[9]

The Synagogue

Have you ever had the good fortune to visit a synagogue? When I was a seventh grader in a Catholic school, I was able to make a visit on a class field trip; and the afternoon I spent at Congregation Shaare

8. *New American Bible.*
9. Vianney Wolfer, *The Prayer of Christ According to the Teaching of St. Thomas Aquinas* (Washington, DC: Catholic University of America Press, 1958), 3.

Emeth was absolutely fascinating.[10] I had no understanding at the time, however, of how the liturgy our hostess described for us went back, in large part, to the centuries before Jesus's birth. The great difference between the synagogue of Jesus's day and the one of today is the absence of the Temple. Today's synagogue is an institution unto itself, whereas the synagogue of Jesus's time was not just spiritually but physically oriented toward the Temple.

When Jesus stood to pray in the synagogue, he and the congregation faced toward Jerusalem. The building was constructed so that the wall they faced as they prayed contained the ark, the repository for the Torah scroll. A curtain hung across the front of the ark, and a lamp was always kept lit, just as in the Temple's Holy of Holies. Between the ark and the congregation was a raised platform with a lectern from which Scripture was proclaimed. In addition to being a place for communal prayer, the synagogue also provided the laity with a rich education in the faith.

The synagogue was active throughout the day. A Jew could visit at any of the three times of prayer to take part in the liturgy. It followed the same pattern as the daily prayer discussed above. So long as ten men were present, one of the laity would lead them in the *Shema* and its blessings, the Eighteen Benedictions, and possibly a psalm.

The great benefit to praying in the synagogue was that after that point in the liturgy, if it was a Sabbath, Monday, or Thursday, then the Torah scroll was taken from the ark and members of the congregation took turns approaching the lectern and reading from it. Because the Torah was in Hebrew and the daily speech of the people Aramaic, the reader paused after each verse as a translator performed his task. Much like today's lectionary, the synagogue made use of a three-year cycle of readings. During morning prayer on the Sabbath, there was an additional reading from the scroll of the Prophets, the *Haftarah*. It was performed by the same member of the laity who led the congregation in the *Shema* and Eighteen Benedictions. When he finished the reading, it was customary for him to

10. See my book *The God Who Is Love: Explaining Christianity from Its Center* (Out of the Box, 2009).

take one of the seats on the raised platform and deliver a sermon. Luke's Gospel recounts a Sabbath when Jesus filled that role (4:16–21).

The scriptural instruction the laity received in the synagogue fed not just the Jewish person's knowledge of God's will but also his prayer. Luke's Gospel shows us how easily the words of Scripture came to Mary's lips in her *Magnificat*:

1 Samuel 2:1–8	Luke 1:46–55
Hannah also prayed and said, "My heart exults in the LORD; my strength is exalted in the LORD. My mouth derides my enemies, because I rejoice in your salvation. There is none holy like the LORD, there is none besides you. . . . The bows of the mighty are broken, but the feeble gird on strength. Those who were full have hired themselves out for bread, but those who were hungry have ceased to be hungry. . . . The LORD makes poor and makes rich; he brings low, he also exalts. He raises up the poor from the dust; he lifts the needy from the dung heap, to make them sit with princes and inherit a seat of honor. . . .	And Mary said, "My soul magnifies the Lord, and my spirit rejoices in God my Savior. . . . holy is his name. And his mercy is on those who fear him from generation to generation. He has shown strength with his arm, he has scattered the proud in the imagination of their hearts, he has brought down the mighty from their thrones, and exalted those of low degree; he has filled the hungry with good things, and the rich he has sent empty away. . . .

The synagogue's liturgy ended with the priestly blessing and the congregation's praying of a brief prayer, the *Qaddish*. If a levitical priest was present, he offered the blessing; but if not, it was read aloud by one of the laity. Many have noted parallels between the *Qaddish* and the *Our Father*—both ask for the sanctification of God and for the establishment of His kingdom on earth: "Magnified and hallowed be his great name in the world that he has created according to his good pleasure; may he cause his kingdom to reign . . . in your lives and in your days and in the lives of the whole house of Israel, very soon and in a near time."[11]

Sabbath Rest

Why did the Lord want His people to keep the Sabbath day holy, to set it apart? "This is a sign between me and you throughout your generations, that you may know that I, the LORD, *sanctify you.* [It is] a perpetual covenant" (Exod. 31:13, 16). The reason God wanted the Jews to avoid work, except in defense of life, from sundown Friday until sundown on Saturday, was to make them holy—a people set apart, a people after His own heart.

Even with the Temple and synagogue liturgies, and stopping three times a day for prayer, God knew that human beings needed still more time for refreshment. They need to break out of their cycle of work and be physically, psychically, and spiritually refreshed. They require time to recollect themselves, to look at those around them, and to truly appreciate their families. The finest meal of the week, prepared the day before so that no one in the house had to labor, was eaten on the Sabbath. If work kept you from visiting the synagogue throughout the week, then at least you had the Sabbath to feast on God's Word, join yourself as a people to the worship of the Temple, and enjoy the fellowship and insights of other members of the congregation. It was as if every week had its own built-in retreat. By divine law, the Jewish people were constantly given a day to stop and appreciate how they, and all they had for life, came from God's hand; and by their obedience, prayer, and union with the Temple sacrifices, they sought to give themselves back to Him.

---

11. John Meier, *A Marginal Jew: Rethinking the Historical Jesus*, Vol. 2 (New York: Doubleday, 1994), 297.

THE CHURCH AT PRAYER

I see the facets of Jesus's prayer we have been considering in this chapter being carried over into our lives in two ways: inside and outside of Mass. In Chapter 2 we looked at how the Temple sacrifices found fulfillment in the Liturgy of the Eucharist. Now we are going to explore how the first half of the Mass, the Liturgy of the Word, continues Jesus's keeping of the Sabbath and worship in the synagogue. We will also see how Jesus's prayer throughout the course of the day and the wearing of *tzitzit*—meant to unite him to the Temple sacrifice—are carried over into prayers like the Liturgy of the Hours and practices like wearing medals, which are meant to connect our daily lives to the Eucharist.

The Lord's Day

Like our Jewish brothers and sisters, we, too, set aside one day of the week for the purpose of worship and rejuvenation. The Jewish Sabbath recalled the rest following God's six days of creation in the book of Genesis, and was celebrated on Saturday, the last day of the week. The early Christians met together to celebrate the Eucharist on the first day of the week (Acts 20:7)—Sunday—the day of Jesus's resurrection. Jesus is the "first fruits" of the new creation, of God's renewal of the world. One of our earliest writings, the *Didache*, or *Teaching of the Twelve Apostles* (written ca. AD 70–120), gave the command: "On *the Lord's* Day of the Lord," meaning Sunday, "gather together, break bread and give thanks...."[12]

The Lord's (Jesus's) Day, or Sunday, is the way Christians participate in Jesus's keeping of the Sabbath, but is meant to go beyond that, too—specifically to open our hearts ever wider to the eternal life that Jesus's death and resurrection have won for us. (CCC 2175) By attending Mass we are inserted into Jesus's Passover from this world to the Father!

---

12. William A. Jurgens, *The Faith of the Early Fathers*, Vol. 1 (Collegeville, MN: The Liturgical Press, 1970), 4.

This crazy, busy world of ours makes our hearts cry out for the Lord's Day. Do you feel run down or distant from God, as if you don't understand your Faith very well, or are barely present to your spouse, children, and friends? Reclaim balance by setting aside Sunday to focus on your relationship with God and the family with which He has blessed you. As Jesus taught, the Sabbath was established for our well-being (Mark 2:27). Strong relationships take time to build and maintain, so making sure you have a day of the week set aside for God, a combination of worship, study, and thought, just makes sense. Spending time with family and beloved friends or making time to help in the community is not a hindrance to this, either; thanks to the Incarnation, the time and love we give to others are given to Jesus himself (Matt. 25:40).

I realize this is difficult to do in our culture, when some jobs force people to work on Sundays. I encourage you to do what you can to celebrate the Lord's Day. With Mass offered Saturday night and both early and late in the day on Sunday, at the bare minimum, make sure your soul gets to feast on the Bread of Life!

Liturgy of the Word

Studying the synagogue has made it obvious where we Catholics received the first half of the Mass. The *Shema* (creed), petitions, the singing of a psalm, readings from the Torah and Prophets, a sermon—it was all there; and it is all still here today. Even the sights remain: the raised platform with the lectern, an ever-burning light kept before the ark, now the tabernacle.

But we Christians take for granted realities unimaginable to the synagogue's faithful. The God-Man is tabernacled not just behind our altars, but within *us*. The Jesus who heard the Father speaking in the Torah and Prophets, whose heart answered in creed, petition, and psalm, does so now through our ears, hearts, and lips. He speaks to us directly through the Gospel reading. We have to ask the Holy Spirit to open the eyes of our heart to recognize these realities and our ears to hear how Jesus's words address *our lives.*

Petition and Intercession

They are the most foundational prayers in existence: Petition—
"God, I need...."—and intercession—"Lord, please help my friend
...." By asking God for our needs and those of our loved ones, we
acknowledge our dependence upon Him, our creaturehood—and
even more, *His Fatherhood.* Even God the Son, in His humanity, peti-
tioned the Father. We heard it combined with blessing and thanksgiving in the Eighteen Benedictions, and in the pages ahead we will
see many other examples. We also noted how Jesus's petitions had
been willed as part of the Incarnation—that the Father had always
willed to bring about salvation through the prayers of His incarnate
Son.

That still holds true, my friends. Our souls were fused to Jesus's
in baptism. When we see our prayers "answered," we haven't
changed God's mind, but have rather conformed ourselves to His
eternal will. He has always had us in mind, always desired to pour
that particular grace into the world out as a result of *our prayer.* We
find this confirmed in the *Catechism:*

Our Father knows what we need before we ask him, but he awaits
our petition because the dignity of his children lies in their
freedom.... Christian prayer is cooperation with his providence,
his plan of love for men.... The prayer of Jesus makes Christian
prayer an efficacious petition. He is its model, he prays in us and
with us. (CCC 2736–2740)

Scapulars and Medals

A cross or crucifix, the Brown Scapular of Our Lady of Mt. Carmel,
the Miraculous Medal, a medal of one's favorite saint worn around
the neck—we Catholics want reminders of our Faith, and the more
visual and tactile the better! It is a way to bring our Lord, his sacrifice, his mother, and saints to mind throughout the day; and when
we do, we can't help but examine ourselves. "*Right now*, am I living
as a child of God?" This was the function of the *tzitzit* that Jewish
men, including Jesus, wore on the corners of their robes.

If we really want to make the most of these holy reminders, we
will offer a prayer when they feel a bit scratchy or catch our attention

in the mirror. If we remove it to shower, then putting it back on can be a renewal of our commitment: "Jesus, I give myself completely to you. As I put on your mother's scapular, I ask to be clothed in her intercession. Give me the grace to say 'yes' to you in everything, just as she did. Keep me moving forward and bring me safely to your Kingdom."

Liturgy of the Hours

I'm sure you've heard of it, but perhaps your personal experience is limited. I'm just wading in myself. What I've found is fascinating, though: "The Liturgy of the Hours ... is the very prayer which Christ himself together with his Body addresses to the Father." (CCC 1174) Also known as the Divine Office, it consists of seven different "hours," or times of prayer.[13] As the "public prayer" of the Church, its purpose is to extend the mysteries of the Incarnation and Passover, present in the Eucharist, throughout the entire day. (CCC 1174)

The psalms have always played the central role. In fact, when the Office was taking shape in sixth-century monasteries, all 150 psalms could be prayed over the course of a single day. At present each hour is made up of a hymn, psalm, a reading from Scripture, and petitions.

Because the psalms for each day are predetermined, we may find them at odds with our own internal state from time to time. That's a good thing, though. It pulls us out of ourselves, allows us to get a better grasp of the fact that we do not come to prayer as "islands." We're peninsulas, at best—always connected to Christ's immense mystical body. If the psalm cries out in pain and need to God, then we do so on behalf of the whole Church; the same is true when we offer thanksgiving and praise. The Holy Spirit widens our hearts, helps us escape the self-centeredness to which we are prone. The Church has always recognized that the psalms were prophetic of Jesus, and that his voice is heard in them. We pray the psalms

---

13. The seven times of prayer were seen as a direct application of Psalm 119:164: "Seven times a day I praise you for your righteous ordinances." Since the Second Vatican Council, however, it has been permissible to eliminate two of the three "little hours" prayed during Day Prayer.

because the body "does not separate itself from its head. It is the one Savior of his body, the Lord Christ Jesus, who prays for us and in us and who is prayed to by us."[14] This explains how we dare to pray words such as those found in Psalm 18: "The LORD rewarded me according to my righteousness; according to the cleanness of my hands he recompensed me" (Ps. 18:20).

While bishops and priests are bound by canon law, and most religious by their constitutions, to daily praying of the Office, the Church strongly recommends it to all her children—as much as our state in life will allow. As I said, I have just started wading in myself.[15] I have found morning prayer (lauds) and evening prayer (vespers) convenient places to start. Mirroring the daily offering in the Temple, morning and evening prayer are the "two hinges on which the daily office turns,"[16] and as such are slightly more detailed hours than the others. Morning prayer always begins, "O God, come to my aid. O Lord, make haste to help me," followed by the *Glory Be*. A hymn and three psalms are then sung or recited. There is a short reading followed by the *Benedictus*, or *Song of Zechariah* (Luke 1:68–79), and intercessions. Morning prayer ends with the *Our Father* and a brief closing prayer. Evening prayer follows the same pattern, but with Mary's *Magnificat* in place of the *Benedictus*.

It's easy to feel a bit intimidated when one discovers how all-encompassing Jewish prayer was in the first century. Once we begin to reflect on the myriad ways we Catholics have to sanctify the day, however, we find that the Jews' robust, continual lifting of the heart to God is alive and well in the Church, especially in the Liturgy of the Hours!

14. *General Instruction of the Liturgy of the Hours*, no. 7, Congregation for Divine Worship, February 2, 1971.

15. Having an iPod and Wi-Fi in the house has made it incredibly convenient; the Office can be accessed online at www.divineoffice.org. You can even listen to it as a podcast.

16. *General Instruction*, no. 37.

4

The Anointed One

Jesus prays before the decisive moments of his mission: before his Father's witness to him during his baptism and . . . his election and call of the Twelve, [and] before Peter's confession of him as "the Christ of God." ∼ CCC 2600

His word and his works are the visible manifestation of his prayer in secret. ∼ CCC 2602

✝

THIS CHAPTER is where we unpack the choice glimpses of Jesus's prayer that we find in the early days of his ministry. We saw our Lord at prayer in the synagogue, but now we see him praying on the banks of the Jordan River and in the wilderness, up on the mountaintops and down on the roads of Galilee. It is the period in which Jesus emerges from the blissful silence of Nazareth and dives headlong into his public role of Messiah, the one "anointed" with the Spirit to bring salvation—to remake hearts so that, like Jesus's, their thoughts, words, actions, and prayer are the action of the Holy Spirit.

JESUS AT PRAYER

On the Banks of the Jordan

"Now when all the people were baptized, and when Jesus also had been baptized [by John] and was praying, the heaven was opened and the Holy Spirit descended upon him in bodily form, as a dove, and a voice came from heaven, 'You are my beloved Son; with you I am well pleased'" (Luke 3:21–22). Mark's Gospel adds to our understanding of the scene by telling us that heaven did not just "open" above Jesus—it was "torn open" (Mark 1:10).[1] Brought together, these two accounts give us the incredible image of the Father tearing heaven apart and pouring out the Holy Spirit upon Jesus, publicly anointing him as the Messiah, all in response to Jesus's *prayer*!

What was it about our Lord's baptism and prayer that called forth such a response? Our baptism as Christians is about washing away original sin, regenerating us as children of God. Jesus had no original sin, no defect of any kind. He was Son of God not by adoption, but by nature. Why then was he baptized? I think the answer to that question will tell us something of the content of Jesus's heaven-rending prayer.

The baptism John administered would not have been a completely foreign sight to Jews of that period. Ritual baths, *mikvahs*, were common among both the Pharisees and Essenes seeking to imitate the purity rituals of priests in the Temple. There are also indications that Gentiles converting to Judaism underwent a "proselyte baptism." John, however, described his baptism as an act of repentance (Matt. 3:11), and it required a public confession of sins (Matt. 3:6). John's God-given task was to ready Israel for the Messiah's appearance. To receive him they would need the humility to let go of their oftentimes distorted vision of life and glory, and receive a new one.

Jesus did not receive baptism for himself, but as the representative of all humanity. Scripture presents him as the new Adam (Rom. 5:18; Mark 1:13), the new head of the human race. As such, he took the weight of his brothers and sisters' failures, their sins, upon himself and makes atonement. Because the world needs to repent of its sins, he leads them in their acts of repentance! Israel had a tradition of leaders confessing sin and asking God for forgiveness in the name of the nation, even when they themselves bore no personal guilt. When the Jews returned after their seventy years of exile in Babylon, their leader Ezra prayed, "I am ashamed and blush to lift my face to you, my God, for our iniquities have risen higher than our heads and our guilt has mounted up to the heavens" (Ezra 9:6). I would

---

1. *New American Bible.*

suggest that this kind of intercession acted as both a reason for Jesus's baptism and a large component of his prayer at the Jordan.

I believe this is corroborated by the words with which the Father responded to him. "You are my beloved Son; with you I am well pleased" is a combination of two different Old Testament passages. The first, Psalm 2:7, "*You are my son,* today I have begotten you," was originally addressed to the Davidic king, and identifies Jesus as the long-awaited Messiah. The second comes from Isaiah 42:1, and alerts us to the unexpected nature of Jesus's messiahship: "Behold my servant, whom I uphold, *my chosen, in whom my soul delights*; I have put my Spirit upon him. . . ." Later in Isaiah we learn that this servant "was oppressed, and he was afflicted, yet he opened not his mouth; like a lamb that is led to the slaughter. [T]he LORD has laid on him the iniquity of us all" (53:7, 6). When John the Baptist identified Jesus to his disciples, it was as "the Lamb of God who takes away the sin of the world!" (John 1:29). I think we're on firm ground in concluding that atoning for humanity's sin was a key theme in Jesus's prayer.

The other theme of Jesus's prayer, the foundation of his every prayer, was also revealed in the Father's response: "You are my beloved Son." Jesus would have prayed, would have shown forth in a human way, who he is within the Trinity—the Son who receives all he is from the Father and pours himself out in a return of love (the Spirit). Even before offering prayers of penitence and confession of his people's sins, Jesus would have been consumed with words of love for his good Father, and *berakah* at the Father sending him to seek and save those who had been lost.

In the Wilderness

The Holy Spirit flowed from Jesus's divinity, through his human heart, and was experienced as a driving force (Mark 1:12), sending him into the desert for forty days of prayer, fasting . . . and temptation. Again, Jesus made atonement for humanity's sins. He relived Adam's experience in the garden and Israel's forty years in the wilderness of Sinai, redeeming their sins through his own acts of faithfulness.(CCC 538–39) He stood strong against Satan's temptations to idolatry, to trying to force the hand of God, and to the lie that a good outcome can ever justify the use of sinful means (Matt. 4:3–11)—temptations responsible for some of humanity's most heinous acts. We should note the way Jesus met each temptation with the words of Scripture. It was right there on the tip of his tongue. It stands to reason that he had contemplated it at length during his forty days. He knew it inside and out and wasn't rattled by Satan's attempt to wrench a verse from its context and use it for his own end.

On the Mountains

Then, just as the Spirit had driven Jesus into the desert, so he called our newly victorious Lord out. "Jesus returned in the power of the Spirit into Galilee" (Luke 4:14). Through the Spirit he preached, taught, healed, exorcised demons (Matt. 4:23–25, 12:28; Luke 5:17), *and he prayed* (Luke 10:21)! In the midst of all that activity, Jesus "would withdraw to deserted places to pray" (Luke 5:16).[2] Even though his every word and action was directed toward establishing his Father's kingdom, the Spirit still moved Jesus to carve out moments of intimacy between himself and the Father; and some of Jesus's favorite spots at which to recollect himself were mountaintops.

Perhaps providentially, my children and I recently returned from a trip to Collinsville, Illinois, to visit Cahokia Mounds. The view from Monks Mound, the highest earthen mound in North America, is fresh in my mind. We could see for miles: green fields and the Mississippi River basin, and through a soft haze the St. Louis Arch and office buildings in the distance. All of us instinctively gasped as we looked out; there is something naturally majestic about such a view. It communicates a sense of awe; and on our good days we let this awe carry our minds and hearts to the one who created such beauty. In this respect, all of Jesus's days were good. The way Jesus—and Old Testament saints like Moses and Elijah—sought out such places to pray teaches us a lesson: Nature can be an aid to prayer.

2. Ibid.

A mountain was where Jesus chose to pray and make one of the most important decisions in history: choosing who would serve as his twelve apostles. He invited the crowd of disciples that had been following him to join his intercession from a distance: "pray therefore the Lord of the harvest to send out laborers into his harvest" (Matt. 9:38). Then he climbed the mountain and "all night he continued in prayer to God" before coming down and selecting the Twelve (Luke 6:12).

A mountaintop—maybe the same one—figured into Jesus's prayer after multiplying the loaves and fishes for the five thousand. Before dismissing the crowds, he instructed the Apostles to sail to the other side of the Sea of Galilee, where he would meet them. After the crowd was on its way, Jesus made the hike up the mountain to pray (Mark 6:46). Jesus kept the three daily times of Jewish prayer, but he went a lot further; the next thing the Gospel tells us is that it's around 3 AM (the "fourth watch") when Jesus saw the Apostles' boat struggling against a strong wind and set out toward them, walking on the water.

The gospels do not tell us the content of Jesus's prayer that night, but Cardinal Ratzinger (later Pope Benedict) made a deduction worthy of Sherlock Holmes: There was no light pollution in the first century, so it would have been pitch black out when Jesus was praying on the mountain; he could not therefore have seen the Apostles' boat struggling with his bodily eyes. Rather, "[i]n his *prayer*, [Jesus] *sees* them. Where Jesus is with the Father, the Church too is present. . . . [T]he Church is, as it were, the subject of conversation between the Father and the Son."[3] I am reminded of the words of Pope Pius XII: "All the members of [Jesus's] Mystical Body were continually and unceasingly present before him. [I]n the crib, on the Cross, in the unending glory of the Father, Christ has all the members of the Church present before him."[4] The Church—you

---

3. Joseph Ratzinger, *The God of Jesus Christ* (San Francisco: Ignatius Press, 2008), 80.

4. Pope Pius XII, *Mystici Corporis Christi* (June 23, 1943). http://www.vatican.va/holy_father/pius_xii/encyclicals/documents/hf_p-xii_enc_29061943_mystici-corporis-christi_en.html.

and I—were the subject of Jesus's prayer here on earth, and we continue to be now that he is in heaven.

Before the Conferral of the Papacy

The papacy is an integral part of the Church, and so we find it being a special focus of Jesus's prayer. Prior to making this study, I had no idea that it was Jesus's prayer that *brought about* Simon-Peter's confession of faith and the conferral of the papacy upon him that we read in Matthew 16:17–19. (CCC 2600) Matthew tells us that Simon's insight into Jesus's identity was a gift from heaven (v. 17); but it is Luke who provides a key piece of background information: It was along the road to Caesarea Philippi, after they had stopped *and Jesus had been at prayer,* that he asked, "Who do people say that I am?" (Luke 9:18). The Father's revelation to Simon was made in response to Jesus's prayer for Simon and the Church.

THE CHURCH AT PRAYER

We saw Jesus anointed with the Spirit at his baptism. Each of us received the Spirit in baptism; he dwells within us. But how do we set him free to reproduce Jesus's prayers, thoughts, words, and actions in us? How do we more perfectly share Jesus's anointing with the Spirit? There is an entire sacrament devoted to just that end.

The Sacrament of Confirmation

In the Acts of the Apostles, the Samaritans who came to believe in Jesus had the exact same need. They became newborns in Christ through the preaching of the deacon Philip and the baptism he administered to them; but something was missing. They received the Holy Spirit in baptism, but the Spirit had not "fallen upon any of them," had not come upon them in the mighty way he came at Pentecost. So what did the Apostles do? Peter and John went to them, and when they "laid their hands" on the Samaritans, "they received the Holy Spirit" (Acts 8:17). How did this laying on of hands change the Samaritans? It introduced them into a deeper participation in Jesus's anointing with the Spirit; and the results must have been pretty spectacular, because a magician actually tried to pay Peter for the power to administer the sacrament (Acts 8:18–24).

If baptism was our conception and birth by the Holy Spirit, allowing us to enter into the mysteries of Jesus's hidden life in Nazareth, then confirmation makes us share his anointing at the Jordan and public life. The grace of confirmation is to participate more fully in the gifts with which the Spirit equipped the Messiah: "the Spirit of the LORD shall rest on him, the spirit of wisdom and understanding, the spirit of counsel and might, the spirit of knowledge and the fear of the Lord [or piety]. And his delight shall be in the fear of the LORD" (Isa. 11:2–3).

I meet a number of Catholic adults who tell me that they didn't come to confirmation with the right attitude, and as a result they do not see where their lives looked any different afterward. Here in the United States, most dioceses administer confirmation at the end of seventh or eighth grade.[5] Some say they were just going through the motions; it was what everyone else their age in the parish did, and it was expected of them. Some even admit to having developed an attachment to some kind of sin—underage drinking, pornography, or possibly premarital sex—with no intention of stopping, sacrament or not. Yes, those kinds of attitudes can definitely block the grace of the sacrament from being realized in someone's life.

The good news, however, is that because confirmation is a sacrament, the grace *is* given. We just need to "stir [it] into flame" (2 Tim. 1:6).[6] This happens when we make a firm decision to turn from sin (and for serious sin that means receiving the sacrament of reconciliation) and sincerely pray, "Jesus, I want to say 'yes' to everything your Holy Spirit wants to do in me. I give you my heart, mind, body, everything that I am. Remove every blockage in my soul and let the gifts of the Spirit come to life in me." And then be prepared—the Lord will begin calling forth the gifts spoken of by

5. Some dioceses administer the sacrament of confirmation at around age seven, prior to First Communion. The "sacraments of initiation" were originally ordered baptism, confirmation, and then Eucharist. Among Eastern Rite Catholics and the Greek Orthodox, *infants* are administered the sacraments in that traditional order.

6. *New American Bible.*

Isaiah. He will put you in situations that call forth the gifts—difficulties where you need knowledge and wisdom, etc. And don't be shocked if, like the Church at Pentecost, you see "charisms," gifts like miracles and tongues, too! (CCC 2003)

The Forty Days of Lent

Each year, between Ash Wednesday and Good Friday, the Church enters into Jesus's forty days in the desert. During his own time there he entered into Israel's forty-year trek; he participated in it and redeemed it. We enter Lent so that that redemption can permeate our lives today.

In the desert our Lord undertook an extreme fast. We enter into it ever so slightly when we follow the Church's discipline of limiting our intake on Ash Wednesday and Good Friday, and forgoing meat on the Fridays of the season. When Jesus fasted, it was a manifestation of what was already within him: the perfect ordering of all his human desires and passions in service to the Father. By grace we want to tap into his discipline and resolve, to discipline our bodies so as to bring about a change of heart.

Our Lenten prayer disposes us to let go of created distractions, good in and of themselves, so that we can better receive the one thing that matters (Luke 10:42). We "give up" something we enjoy. We want to be able to honestly say, along with Jesus, "My food is to do the will of him who sent me, and to accomplish his work" (John 4:34).

Making a Retreat

Jesus made a habit of carving out private time away from the crowds and the demands of his busy life to pray. He knew the Apostles needed that, too: "Come away by yourselves to a lonely place, and rest a while" (Mark 6:31). Jesus makes the same invitation to you—to carve out a weekend, a day, or even just a few hours one evening in which to break away and join him in focusing upon the Father.

There is such a variety of retreat experiences available to us: week-long silent retreats in a monastery, weekend Christ Renews

His Parish retreats and Life in the Spirit seminars. Most parishes have a yearly mission that runs for three or four nights, and some offer periodic evenings of recollection as well.

For me, retreats are often "mountaintop" experiences. Away from the frustrations experienced at school or work, a peaceful space is created where God can really get my attention and renew my outlook. Physically, emotionally, and spiritually, I feel on top of the world.

Jesus knew the "mountaintop" experience—figuratively and literally! It is valuable; but Jesus did not spend his life on the mountain. He broke away from the daily grind and went up to the heights to commune with the Father, but he did not forget the world. His Church was always there in his conversation with the Father. He came down from the mountain recharged to live out his vocation among God's people—frustrating, tiring people, just like the ones surrounding you and me—*just like* you and me.

5

The Teacher

[We] approach the holy Lord Jesus as Moses approached the burning bush; first to contemplate him in prayer, then to hear how he teaches us to pray.... ⁓CCC 2598

Run through all the words of the holy prayers [in Scripture], and I do not think you will find anything in them that is not contained and included in the Lord's Prayer. ⁓St. Augustine, CCC 2762

✝

HERE WE WILL STUDY the teachings Jesus gave on prayer to the crowds of Galilee and Judea. Jesus's instruction comes under three general headings: 1) the attitudes we should bring to prayer; 2) the prayer Jesus taught us, the *Our Father*; and 3) the actions that should accompany prayer. Then in the final portion of the chapter, we will explore the means Jesus gives us for living his teaching in the Church today.

THE TEACHING OF JESUS
PART I: ATTITUDES

The right attitude makes all the difference, doesn't it? Jesus seems to have thought so, because the majority of his instruction on prayer has to do with our disposition. Prayer isn't a matter of choosing the perfect words, but of our hearts being able to commune with God. Jesus was "gentle and lowly in heart" (Matt. 11:29), and he expects us to approach the Father in the same way.

44

Thanksgiving

We have seen how *berakah*, thanksgiving and blessing, acts as the foundation of Jewish prayer. Although Jesus did not explicitly teach the necessity of grounding our prayer in it, he exemplified it in his own prayer (Luke 10:21; Mark 6:41; John 11:41–42; Matt. 26:26–28); and he drew attention to it when it was lacking (Luke 17:11–19). Ironically, giving thanks makes *me* feel enriched; I realize how lavishly God loves and provides for me in Christ.

Humility

Thanksgiving for what we have received—and that is literally *everything*, even our existence—means that we must approach God in humility. It was our Blessed Mother's attitude (Luke 1:48), and her greatness is second only to Jesus's. It was the attitude of Jesus himself.[1]

We do well to recall the parable our Lord told to "some who trusted in themselves that they were righteous and despised others." Both a Pharisee and tax collector went up to the Temple. The Pharisee prayed aloud for all to hear, giving thanks—thanks for how much better he was than all of the sinners. The tax collector, on the other hand, understood the depth of human need, and his need in particular; with downcast eyes, he "beat his breast, saying 'God, be merciful to me a sinner!'" (Luke 18:9–14). Care to guess which one went home right with God?

The Pharisee of the parable illustrates something of which Jesus greatly disapproved: those who wish to exploit their religion, to "use" God for their own selfish ends. He tells us, "Beware of practicing your piety before men in order to be seen by them; for then you will have no reward from your Father who is in heaven. [Instead,] go into your room and shut the door and pray to your Father who is in secret; and your Father who sees in secret will reward you" (Matt. 6:1, 6). As we will shortly see, this wasn't meant to rule out communal prayer, but rather to drive home the point that prayer is to be a loving communication with the Divine, not a self-centered, self-serving monologue.

---

1. See Matt. 11:29; John 13:3–17; and Phil. 2:3–11.

Faith

Faith is an absolute prerequisite in approaching God. Jesus wants us to display the same faith, the same confidence in the Father, Son, and Holy Spirit's power that the centurion did so long ago in Capernaum: "only say the word, and my servant will be healed (Matt. 8:8). We should have faith not only in God's power but also in His tender love and desire to provide for us:

> Therefore I tell you, do not be anxious about your life, what you shall eat or what you shall drink, nor about your body, what you shall put on. [Y]our heavenly Father knows that you need them all. (Matt. 6:25–33)

> Ask, and it will be given you; seek, and you will find; knock, and it will be opened to you. [W]hat man of you, if his son asks him for bread, will give him a stone? ... If you then, who are evil, know how to give good gifts to your children, how much more will your Father who is in heaven give good things to those who ask him! (Matt. 7:7–12)

> If you then, who are evil, know how to give good gifts to your children, how much more will the heavenly Father give the Holy Spirit to those who ask him! (Luke 11:13)

God wants us to ask for what we need; it was part of His plan that *Jesus ask*! Some graces are poured out only in response to the prayer of Jesus and his Church.[2]

God's Fatherly love gives us the proper context for understanding passages like Mark 11:22–24: "Therefore I tell you, whatever you ask in prayer, believe that you receive it, and you will." Because God is our Father, Jesus's words implicitly contain the caveat made by every good parent: "When the time is right, and so long as it is good for you."

---

2. One of the ways Jesus builds up his body is by promising a special blessing on prayers offered in common. "[I]f two of you agree on earth about anything they ask, it will be done for them by my Father in heaven. For where two or three are gathered in my name, there am I in the midst of them" (Matt. 18:19–20).

Persistence

Because our requests are answered according to God's knowledge and wisdom instead of ours, we need to be prepared for the "long haul." Jesus told two parables, both quite funny, to illustrate the persistence we need to have in prayer. The first was about a man whose friend came knocking on the door at midnight, wanting to borrow some food. At first the man told him to take a hike; but when the friend continued knocking, the man finally got out of bed and gave him what he needed (Luke 11:5–8). The second parable had to do with a widow pestering a judge over her case. Even though this judge was a man who "neither feared God nor regarded man," she finally wore him down to the point of ruling in her favor. Jesus ended the parable by asking, "And will not God vindicate his elect, who cry to him day and night? Will he delay long over them? I tell you, he will vindicate them speedily" (Luke 18:1–8).

The gospels give us an example of how effective such persistence is. When a Syro-Phoenician woman whose daughter was possessed came to Jesus and asked him to expel the demon, he appeared to refuse her. "It is not fair to take the children's [Israel's] bread and throw it to the dogs [the Gentiles]." Far from crushing the woman's faith, it called forth even more. "Yes, Lord, yet even the dogs eat the crumbs that fall from their master's table." Jesus marveled at her. "O woman, great is your faith! Let it be done for you as you desire." And her daughter was healed instantly (Matt. 15:26–28). Persistently making our needs known to God exercises our faith.

You and I are guaranteed a share of difficult times (Sir. 2:1–19). When they stretch on, we may be tempted to feel that God is not listening to us; but nothing could be further from the truth. Our Father is already at work behind the scenes, and as with the Syro-Phoenician woman, his delay is calling forth the gift of faith from our souls. This is the truth that moved St. Paul to write, "we rejoice in our sufferings, knowing that suffering produces endurance, and endurance produces character, and character produces hope, and hope does not disappoint us, because God's love has been poured into our hearts through the Holy Spirit who has been given to us" (Rom. 5:3–5). Persistence in prayer calls us into deep spiritual waters; God has told us how the story ends—our every need and desire fulfilled beyond our wildest imaginings. Knowing this, we come to prayer with hearts full of thanks, humble in our need, confident in his power and love, and persistent in our communion with him.

PART II: THE PRAYER JESUS TAUGHT US

When I first became serious about my relationship with God, I did not like using "canned" prayers like the *Our Father* and *Hail Mary*. I grew up going to Catholic school and said these prayers for years without God being my personal center—that was me. So when I had an intense personal encounter with Jesus, I tended to devalue everything that had come before. Those "cookie-cutter, pre-made" prayers I prayed in childhood hadn't affected me the way I thought they should, and so I began offering only spontaneous, conversational prayers.

As the years passed, however, God opened my eyes and heart to some important realizations. First, I began to notice how everything I was trying to put into my spontaneous prayer, *and more*, was already there in the *Our Father*: praise and thanksgiving; the conversion of loved ones; that the world at large begin doing things God's way; all of my and my loved ones' bodily, emotional, and spiritual needs; forgiveness; the strength I needed to overcome sin; and deliverance from all manner of evil. The *Our Father* was a complete school of prayer. Why that would surprise me, I do not know—as if I could ever improve on God the Son's prayer!

My final realization came as I more deeply penetrated the core of our Faith: that Jesus is living his life *in us* (Col. 1:27). Through the Spirit, he uses our lips to speak his words (Mark 13:11), our actions to express his love (Eph. 2:10), and even our prayers to manifest his own communication with the Father. That's not just Cardinal Ratzinger or Shane Kapler's speculation—that's the teaching of Scripture. "God sent the Spirit of his Son into our hearts, crying out 'Abba! Father!'" (Gal. 4:6). That is what happens when we pray the *Our Father*! But until following Jesus became the most important thing in my life, I do not know that I had ever prayed the *Our Father* from my *heart*, that inner sanctum where the Spirit had resided since baptism.

If you have read this far, then you have probably already made a personal commitment to following Jesus as your Lord, as the master of your entire life. And if so, then your heart should be fertile ground for the *Our Father* to take root and propel your spiritual growth. We find it in both Luke and Matthew:

Luke 11:1–4	Matthew 6:7–13
He was praying in a certain place, and when he ceased, one of his disciples said to him, "Lord, teach us to pray. . . ." And he said to them, "When you pray, say:	And in praying do not heap up empty phrases as the Gentiles do. [Y]our Father knows what you need before you ask him. Pray then like this:
'Father, hallowed be thy name. Thy kingdom come.	Our Father who art in heaven, Hallowed be thy name. Thy kingdom come. Thy will be done, On earth as it is in heaven.
Give us each day our daily bread; and forgive us our sins, for we ourselves forgive every one who is indebted to us; and lead us not into temptation.'"	Give us this day our daily bread; And forgive us our trespasses, As we forgive those who trespass against us; And lead us not into temptation, But deliver us from evil.

Matthew's introduction gives the impression that Jesus meant for this prayer to get right to the heart of things. So why then is Matthew's version longer than Luke's? Different reasons have been suggested: Matthew wrote his Gospel for a primarily Jewish audience, and there were certain expectations regarding style.[3] When we look at the Psalms, for instance, we see parallelism; a thought is repeated and slightly intensified in the following line. This may explain Matthew's "Thy kingdom come. Thy will be done on earth, as it is in heaven" in lieu of Luke's brief "Thy kingdom come." There is no change in meaning from one Gospel to the other, only an unfolding of the intent. The same would hold true for the end of the prayer:

3. Benedict Vivian, "The Gospel According to Matthew," in *The New Jerome Biblical Commentary*, ed. R.E. Brown, J.A. Fitzmeyer, and R.E. Murphy (Englewood Cliffs, NJ: Prentice Hall, 1990), 640, 645.

"and lead us not into temptation." Matthew's Gospel might also record Jesus's own later elaboration on the shorter version recorded in Luke. If that is the case, then each form came directly from the mouth of Jesus, but on two separate occasions. For the sake of harvesting as many riches as we can, and letting Tradition be our guide, we will reflect upon the slightly longer version found in Matthew.

Our Father, Who Art in Heaven

Abba: It was always Jesus's address for God. It was the Aramaic word little children used for "Daddy" or "Papa," and the way adult children tenderly and reverently addressed a beloved father.[4] I cannot help but imagine its being the only word that escaped his lips during some of those long nights on the mountain or in the desert. While addressing God as Father wasn't unknown in Jewish prayer, it was rare. When it was used, it meant simply that God was *like* a father (e.g., Psalm 103). When Jesus, on the other hand, said "Father," he meant it literally; he is God's Son *by nature*.

What makes the *Our Father* such an earth-shattering prayer is that the Son invites us to say "*our* Father!" In baptism, Jesus made us "participants of the divine nature" (2 Pet. 1:4). "When we cry, 'Abba! Father!' it is the Spirit himself bearing witness with our spirit that we are children of God" (Rom. 8:15–16). This is *berakah*. The first words of our prayer are ones of awe and thanksgiving for the unmerited gifts of our existence and adoption into God's family.

Addressing God as "our" Father also reminds us that there is no such thing as a spiritual Lone Ranger. We come to the Father as part of an immense family that stretches from heaven to earth (Eph. 3:15). We pray as members of his Son, manifesting the reality we saw in the last chapter, that the Church is always there with Jesus in his prayers to the Father. Each of the petitions we make in the *Our Father* are made for the body as a whole.

By praying to our Father "who art in heaven," we gratefully recognize that God's Fatherhood differs from human fatherhood. We

---

4. Paul Hinnebusch, *The Lord's Prayer in the Light of Our Lord's Life and Preaching* (Boston: Pauline Books & Media, 1996), 17–18.

do not have to compete with the demands of work or a football game for this Father's attention, nor can we manipulate Him to get our way. In God we have pure, infinite, non-attenuated Fatherhood, of which even the best on earth is a pale reflection.

Hallowed Be Thy Name

We pray that God will cause His Name to be reverenced in the world. It is a petition for conversion of heart, both ours and the world's. We're asking God to fulfill His promise: "It is not for your sake, O house of Israel, that I am about to act, but for the sake of my holy name, which you have profaned among the nations to which you came. . . . A new heart I will give you, and a new spirit I will put within you . . . and cause you to walk in my statutes" (Ezek. 36:22–27). We are praying for the grace to yield to the Holy Spirit as Jesus did, even in the face of great trials. Jesus prayed this very petition just days before his crucifixion: "And what shall I say? 'Father, save me from this hour'? No, for this purpose I have come to this hour. *'Father, glorify thy name.'* Then a voice came from heaven, 'I have glorified it, and I will glorify it again'" (John 12:27–28). Jesus's faithfulness to the Father brought more glory to God's Name than all other acts in human history combined. Jesus wants to continue glorifying the Father by reproducing his faithfulness in us.

Thy Kingdom Come

"Kingdom" is our English translation of Matthew and Luke's Greek term *basileia*. It refers to "the regal function, the *active lordship* of the king."[5] Ultimately what we're asking for in this petition is for Jesus to return as judge and for God's rule to be established in power. As we await that final day, this petition asks that God's rule will be established in both our hearts and others throughout the world. We pray for God's Law, which recognizes the innate dignity and sanctity of every life, to become the law of man.

---

5. Benedict XVI, *Jesus of Nazareth: From the Baptism in the Jordan to the Transfiguration* (New York: Doubleday, 2007), 55. See also CCC 2816.

Thy Will Be Done, on Earth As It Is in Heaven

This petition is an amplification of the previous petition. It makes us look to the example of the angels, who execute God's will perfectly and without hesitation. Even higher than the angels, though, our eyes go to Jesus who called doing the Father's will his "food" (John 4:34). What is God's will for us? To join ourselves to Jesus and live his life—to live the *Shema* and the Ten Commandments, and to love our neighbors as ourselves by performing works of loving kindness (Matt. 19:17–22; Mark 12:28–34; John 13:34). This petition calls out for that grace. (CCC 2825) It asks this grace for the entire world, and in a special way for those charged with governance—that we be able to exercise our faith without hindrance (1 Tim. 2:1–4).

Give Us This Day Our Daily Bread

This petition seems quite straightforward, a prayer for sustenance. In "daily bread" we hear an echo from Israel's days in the wilderness, when the Lord sent manna at the start of each new day. After the people had gathered as much as they could eat and the sun grew hot, it melted (Exod. 16:4–21). If the Israelites were anything like me, they would much rather have gathered in a week's worth at once. As it was, not only were the Israelites spared the threat of expanding waistlines, but they stayed humble; as the book of Proverbs says, "give me neither poverty nor riches; feed me with the food that is needful for me, lest I be full, and deny you, and say, 'Who is the LORD?' or lest I be poor, and steal, and profane the name of my God" (Prov. 30:8–9).

Besides recalling the experiences and wisdom of the Old Testament, this petition recalls Jesus's teaching on practical faith: "do not be anxious about your life, what you shall eat or what you shall drink, nor about your body, what you shall put on. [Y]our heavenly Father knows that you need them all. . . . Ask, and it will be given you. . . ." (Matt. 6:25, 32; 7:7).

As we pray this petition, we should be sensitive to how God may want to use us to answer someone else's prayer. If we are aware of someone's need and have the ability to meet it, then we are under an obligation to do so (James 2:15–17).

This petition of the Lord's Prayer is very special in that there is a second level of meaning the saints recognized early on. The Greek word we translate as "daily" is *epiousios*. If we divide the word differently—as *epi-ousios*—it can be translated "super-essential" or "super-substantial." (CCC 2837) What makes translation of this adjective so intriguing is that it occurs nowhere else in all of Greek literature.[6] Because of this the Fathers of the Church were almost unanimous in understanding the *Our Father* to petition God for the true daily bread, the "super-substantial" bread of the Eucharist.[7] The daily bread that was given to the Israelites was a foreshadowing, but Jesus in the Eucharist is the reality (John 6:49–51)!

The wonderful truth is that we don't have to choose between these two levels of meaning when we pray the *Our Father*.[8] All our bodily and spiritual needs are captured in that one petition.

Forgive Us Our Trespasses, As We Forgive Those Who Trespass Against Us

It is a tremendous comfort to know that while our sins and failings are often a surprise to us, Jesus already took them into account. He knew that each time we approach the Father we need to ask forgiveness for something. The first half of this petition flows from us naturally.

It is the second half of the petition, the part about forgiving others, that gives us trouble. Jesus knew it, and that's why after he finished the *Our Father*, the next words out of his mouth were, "For if you forgive men their trespasses, your heavenly Father also will forgive you; but if you do not forgive men their trespasses, neither will your Father forgive your trespasses" (Matt. 6:14–15). He drove home the point two other times in the Sermon on the Mount (Matt. 5:24, 5:44) and again later in the parable of the unmerciful servant (Matt. 18:32–35).

It is hard, though; forgiving others might be the hardest thing we

---

6. Scott Hahn, *Understanding "Our Father": Biblical Reflections on the Lord's Prayer* (Steubenville, OH: Emmaus Road Publishing, 2002), 46.

7. Benedict XVI, *Jesus of Nazareth*, 153–54.

8. Hahn, *Understanding "Our Father"*.

Christians do. Sometimes the hurt is so deep that our prayer can only be a baby step: "Lord, *let me want* to forgive him," or even, "Lord, let me want *to want* to forgive him." The Catechism doesn't sugarcoat it, but it does point the way to victory:

> Only the Spirit by whom we live can make "ours" the same mind that was in Christ Jesus. [I]t is not in our power not to feel or to forget an offense; but the heart that offers itself to the Holy Spirit turns injury into compassion and purifies the memory in transforming the hurt into intercession. (CCC 2842–3)

And Lead Us Not into Temptation

The wording of this petition, at least in English, is a tad confusing. Elsewhere the Bible says that temptations do not come from God (James 1:13). Going back to the original Greek helps us to see that what Jesus wants us to pray for is the grace: a) to avoid the situations that make it easier to yield to temptation, and b) when tempted, to stand our ground. (CCC 2846) God is a good Father, so He doesn't create situations to try and make us fall.

There is a difference, however, between temptations and trials. Our Father does have a role in the latter. Trials are the "resistance training" of the spiritual life, requiring us to exert ourselves to overcome a difficulty. "My son, when you come to serve the LORD, prepare yourself for trials. . . . Cling to him, forsake him not; thus will your future be great" (Sir. 2:1, 3). Saint Paul explains why this is so: "endurance produces character, and character produces hope, and hope does not disappoint us, because God's love has been poured into our hearts through the Holy Spirit which has been given to us" (Rom. 5:3–5). Trials force us to "dig deep" and cultivate the theological virtues deposited in our souls at baptism: faith, hope, and love.

Our natural lives are a series of trials. What was school, if not a series of trials (a.k.a., "tests") forcing you to grapple with and apply the information imparted by your teachers? If you played a sport, then I bet your coach put you through a series of trials (a.k.a., "practices") before a competition. And if it's been a while since you graduated or competed, you know what happens to skills when they are no longer periodically "put to the test"—they disappear!

God allows us to go through trials with a positive end in mind, but they are not without their dangers. When we go through a stressful trial, we can be *especially susceptible to the temptations* that surround us; and we can give in to them, either as an illicit way to resolve the situation or as a momentary escape from stress. A husband passing through a difficult season in his marriage, for example, may find himself tempted by the flirtations of an attractive, vivacious coworker. The difficulties associated with life at home, paying the mortgage and running children to activities, do not exist with the coworker. If he stays the course and works through the difficulties at home, then God will bring him to even deeper levels of love and communication with his wife, and a deeper experience of Christian manhood (Eph. 5:25–33). If he turns away to pursue someone new, however, he will shipwreck his faith and do untold damage to his family.

We can understand why Jesus taught us to petition the Father for the grace to overcome temptation! As we pass through our daily lives, and especially in times of trial, we need God's grace to overcome the temptations put to us from the devil (more on him shortly), the fallen world in which we live, and our own weakness. No matter what we are facing, we should never despair; our Father wants us to overcome. "No testing has overtaken you that is not common to everyone. God is faithful, and he will not let you be tested beyond your strength, but with the testing he will provide the way out so that you may be able to endure it" (1 Cor. 10:13).

We will find this especially true in our world's final days. Before Jesus returns, the Church will be persecuted like never before. People will be tempted to escape from it by renouncing the Faith. Jesus told the Apostles the secret to standing strong: "Be alert at all times, *praying that you may have strength* to escape all these things that will take place, and to stand before the Son of man" (Luke 21:36). Those who faithfully pray the *Our Father*, who call out for God's grace to remain strong, will take on the image of Christ and manifest his Passion before the eyes of the world—and then Jesus will return to share his resurrection with them.[9]

9. See CCC 675–77.

But Deliver Us from Evil

Here we intensify the cry from the previous petition. In English it is traditional for us to pray "deliver us from evil"; but Jesus literally said, "deliver us from the evil one." (Matt. 6:13; CCC 2851) That's right—there is a devil out there; and he is gunning for you. If you think that thought is antiquated or childish, then he's got you right where he wants you—completely oblivious to his activity. Jesus doesn't mean for you to walk around in mortal fear, but to recognize your enemy and to petition the Father for the grace to overcome him, especially in your weakest moments, when you are passing through trials. Listen to St. Peter's advice:

> Discipline yourselves, keep alert. Like a roaring lion your adversary the devil prowls around, looking for someone to devour. Resist him, steadfast in your faith, for you know that your brothers and sisters in all the world are undergoing the same kinds of suffering. And after you have suffered for a little while, the God of all grace, who has called you to his eternal glory in Christ, will himself restore, support, strengthen, and establish you. (1 Peter 5:8–10)

As children we cry out for our Father to deal with this threat, absolutely confident that He will.

Doxology: For the Kingdom, the Power, and the Glory Are Yours, Now and Forever

A Protestant friend once asked me why Catholics leave off the end of the Lord's Prayer. The answer is surprising: It's not that Catholics leave it off, but that most other Christians add it on. The earliest biblical manuscripts do not have those words at the end of the prayer (Matt. 6:13; Luke 11:4).[10] They have become forever linked to the Lord's Prayer, though, because they follow it in the Mass. At the time of the Reformation, they were mistakenly retained as the prayer's culmination by those separating from the Catholic Church.

---

10. We find "For thine is the power and the glory forever" in the *Didache*, written AD 70–120, and the full doxology in the late third-century work *The Apostolic Constitutions*.

Concluding Thoughts

There are those who believe the *Our Father* to be Jesus's condensation of the Eighteen Benedictions or his reworking of the *Qaddish* prayer. The *Didache*, Christianity's first catechism (AD 70–120), taught that the *Our Father* should be prayed three times a day, just like the Eighteen Benedictions (CCC 2767), and the *Qaddish* does pray for the magnification and holiness of God's Name as well as the establishment of His kingdom. We do find these thoughts in the *Our Father*—a thoroughly Jewish prayer, delivered by a thoroughly Jewish Messiah. The fact of the matter is that the *Our Father* summarizes *every other prayer*. Its seven petitions capture every need of humanity. That shouldn't surprise us—consider the Teacher!

One last question to ask: The *Our Father* is the chief prayer of the body, but was it the prayer of the Head as well? Did Jesus pray the *Our Father*? When the question was first put to me many years ago, it seemed completely inappropriate; how could Jesus pray "Forgive us our trespasses?" And yet, as I later learned, that was exactly what his actions said when he submitted to John's baptism. He can ask forgiveness as a human being, *on behalf of his sinful brothers and sisters*—"Forgive us *our* trespasses." As the prayer of Jesus—offered on behalf of, as well as in union with, his Church—I cannot think of an objection to the idea that it was truly "the *Lord's* Prayer."

Let's conclude with the words of the *Catechism*:

> The prayer that comes to us from Jesus is truly unique. . . . On the one hand, in the words of this prayer the only Son gives us the words the Father gave him [John 17:7]. . . . On the other, as Word incarnate, he knows in his human heart the needs of his human brothers and sisters and reveals them to us. . . . (CCC 2765)

PART III: ACTIONS TO ACCOMPANY PRAYER

The Talmud attributes a famous saying to Simeon the Righteous (the high priest memorialized in Sirach 50:1–21). It says that the world stands on three things: *Torah* (the Law found in Scripture), *avodah* (sacrificial worship), and *gemilut chasadim* (acts of loving kindness). We have seen the part that the first two elements played in Jesus's prayer life, and Jesus's teaching shows that he considered the third element a "given" as well. In the Sermon on the Mount, the *Our Father* is placed between Jesus's teaching on almsgiving and fasting. Neither practice was optional in his mind; it was never a matter of "if" his disciples would engage in them, but of when and how (Matt. 6:2, 16).

Almsgiving

Care of the poor had always been part of Mosaic Law. When harvesting, for example, Israelite farmers were ordered to leave a portion of the field untouched, so that the poor could come and gather what they needed (Lev. 19:9–10, 23:22; Deut. 24:19–22). The deuterocanonical books Tobit and Sirach, written in the centuries just before Jesus's birth, put a tremendous value on almsgiving. We can see how Jesus drew from Sirach in his own teaching:

Sirach 29:10–13	Luke 12:32–34
Lose your silver for the sake of a brother or a friend, and do not let it rust under a stone and be lost. Lay up your treasure according to the commandments of the Most High, and it will profit you more than gold. Store up almsgiving in your treasury, and it will rescue you from every disaster; better than a stout shield and a sturdy spear, it will fight for you against the enemy.	Sell your possessions, and give alms; provide yourselves with purses that do not grow old, with a treasure in the heavens that does not fail, where no thief approaches and no moth destroys. For where your treasure is, there will your heart be also.

Because it is a religious act, Jesus commanded that, just as with prayer, alms not be given to win esteem from others. "But when you give alms, do not let your left hand know what your right hand is doing, so that your alms may be in secret; and your Father who sees in secret will reward you" (Matt. 6:3–4). Impure motives nullify the gift's value in God's eyes. This was what Jesus saw happening with many among the Pharisees (Luke 11:41–42).

The New Testament gives us a wonderful example with which to contrast the behavior of the Pharisee: the Roman centurion Cornelius, the first gentile admitted to the Church. He had come to believe in the God of Israel and "gave alms liberally to the people, and prayed constantly to God" (Acts 10:2). Because of that, an angel was sent to him with the message, "Your *prayers and your alms have ascended as a memorial* before God. Now send men to Joppa for a certain Simon who is called Peter" (10:4–5). Did you catch the way the angel worded that? God received Cornelius's prayers and acts of loving kindness as *sacrificial offerings*, and God reciprocated by having the Good News revealed to him. Cornelius's cooperation with God's grace to pray and give alms to the poor had been built into God's plan. It was that final, infinitesimal turning of the key that God had ordained for unlocking the floodgates of Christ's grace to all the other nations of the world! It should make us wonder what mighty purpose(s) God has pre-ordained for *our* prayers and actions.

Jesus has already revealed the ultimate purpose of these acts: love of God. Because God became incarnate, Jesus could teach, "as you did it to one of the least of these who are members of my [human] family, you did it to me.... I was hungry and you gave me food ... thirsty, and you gave me something to drink ... a stranger and you welcomed me ... naked and you gave me clothing ... sick and you took care of me ... in prison and you visited me" (Matt. 25:40, 35–36).

Fasting

In the Sermon on the Mount, Jesus addressed the need for not just prayer and almsgiving, but fasting. The three were intimately connected in the Jewish mind (Tob. 12:8). The great heroes of the Old Testament espoused fasting: Moses (Exod. 24:18; Deut. 9:9), Samuel (1 Sam. 7:1–6), David (2 Sam. 12:15–17), Judas Maccabeus (1 Macc. 3:42–53), and let's not forget how the city of Nineveh was spared because of its fast (Jon. 3:4–10). The Law required a twenty-four hour fast on the Day of Atonement (Lev. 23:27–29); and following the exile, the Jews adopted four other annual days of fasting, as well (Zech. 8:19). The Pharisees fasted two days a week: Mondays and Thursdays (Luke 18:12). It was a concrete way of telling God, "You alone are our hope and sustenance."

Sadly, abuses arose. Some began to look at fasting as something mechanical, as if it bound God to pouring out His blessings, even in the face of gross sin. The Old Testament prophets took great exception to that attitude (Joel 2:12; Isa. 58:3–9). Jesus reminded his listeners that fasting was meant to increase the soul's intimacy with God, not win human praise. "[W]hen you fast, anoint your head and wash your face, that your fasting may be seen not by men but by your Father who is in secret; and your Father who sees in secret will reward you" (Matt. 6:17–18).

Fasting was part of Jesus's life and was a regular practice in the early Church, too.[11] Fasting and prayer preceded the revelation that Paul and Barnabas were to be sent out as missionaries (Acts 13:1–3) as well as Paul and Barnabas's ordination of presbyters (priests) in the communities they founded (Acts 14:23). Paul wrote of the value it and other mortifications played in his life: "Every athlete exercises self-control in all things. They do it to receive a perishable wreath, but we an imperishable. Well, I do not run aimlessly, I do not box as one beating the air; but I pommel my body and subdue it, lest after preaching to others I myself should be disqualified" (1 Cor. 9:25–27). In the third century, we read of Christians fasting twice a week: Wednesdays and Fridays.

In summary, Jesus taught his Church that prayer engaged the whole person—the mind and lips presenting the fruit of a well-disposed heart, and mounting up to heaven on wings fashioned from acts of loving kindness and mortifications.

THE CHURCH AT PRAYER

Prayer, acts of loving kindness like almsgiving, and fasting are of course plentiful in the Church today. I am going to limit myself to three traditional forms to share with you: using the *Our Father* as a

---

11. We do not hear of the Apostles fasting during Jesus's public ministry. When questioned about it, Jesus answered the disciples of the Baptist and Pharisees, "Can you make wedding guests fast while the bridegroom is with them? The days will come, when the bridegroom is taken away from them, and then they will fast in those days" (Luke 5:34–35).

template for prayer, the corporal and spiritual works of mercy, and abstinence from meat/fasting on Ash Wednesday, Good Friday, and the Fridays of Lent.

The *Our Father* As a Template

Because the *Our Father* is the perfect prayer, we can use it as a model, a pattern, for personal times of prayer. We can fill each line with our own thanks and petitions. Allow me to offer a few suggestions:

Our Father who art in heaven: Praise the qualities of God of which you are most cognizant, and thank Him for favors and the many ways He has shown His care to you and your loved ones (family life, housing, friendships, employment, and so forth).

Hallowed be thy name: Pray for atheists, agnostics, and anyone you know who is not practicing his/her faith.

Thy kingdom come: Intercede for the needs you hear on your national and local news. Pray that abortion be outlawed and marriage respected.

Thy will be done on earth as it is in heaven: Mention your family, friends, coworkers, and clergy.

Give us this day our daily bread: Pray for your needs and those of the people around you.

Forgive us our trespasses: Confess your sins and ask God's forgiveness for others of whose sin you are aware.

As we forgive those who trespass against us: Ask God for the grace to forgive, both for yourself and others who have been wronged.

And lead us not into temptation: Petition God to help you and others in your weakest areas.

But deliver us from evil: Ask God to protect you and those in your family and community from the evils you fear.

A shorter variation is to visualize the faces and situations that correspond to each petition as you recite the *Our Father*, asking Jesus and the Spirit to provide whatever might be lacking on your part (Rom. 8:26–27).

The Corporal (Bodily) and Spiritual Works of Mercy

Do you want to become a saint? Are you looking for concrete ways to "Love your neighbor as yourself"? The Church combed the New Testament long ago and composed two lists of *gemilut chasadim* (acts of loving kindness):[12]

Corporal Works of Mercy	Spiritual Works of Mercy
Feed the hungry	Counsel the doubtful
Give drink to the thirsty	Instruct the ignorant
Clothe the naked	Admonish the sinner
Welcome the stranger	Comfort the sorrowful
Visit the sick and imprisoned	Bear wrongs patiently
Bury the dead	Pray for the living and the dead

If those intimidate you (although they shouldn't—the Holy Spirit lives inside of you, after all), then the Church has composed a bare-bones list of what actions should accompany membership in Christ's Catholic Church. They are known as the Precepts of the Church (CCC 2041–42): (1) Attend Mass on Sundays and holy days of obligation; (2) Make a sacramental confession at least once a year; (3) Receive the Eucharist during the Easter season; (4) Observe the Church's days of fasting and abstinence; and (5) Help provide for the material needs of the Church.

Ash Wednesday, Good Friday, and the Fridays of Lent

We are going to unpack precept number four above. Abstinence from meat during the Fridays of Lent is one of the cultural hallmarks of today's Catholic. On Ash Wednesday and Good Friday, not only do we abstain from meat—we also limit ourselves to one regular-sized meal and two snacks. (Neither of the snacks, when added together, should equal the size of a second meal.)

There is of course nothing *objectively* wrong or sinful in consuming meat or regular-sized meals on a Friday. Rather, the Church is

---

12. CCC 2447.

invoking her spiritual authority over us and calling us to a small participation in the fasting Jesus has prescribed for us. She has the authority to ask this of us, and it would be wrong to refuse her. As Jesus said to her first leaders, "whatever you bind on earth shall be bound in heaven" (Matt. 18:18). When we fast and abstain from meat, we should do it in the way Jesus told us to, the way he himself did—without drawing attention to ourselves, as an act of love for our Father in heaven.

6

Transfigured:
Illuminating the Inner Life

Jesus prays before the decisive moments of his mission: before his Father's witness to him during his . . . Transfiguration. CCC 2600

By contemplating and hearing the Son, the master of prayer, the children learn to pray to the Father. CCC 2601

✝

WE LOOKED AT the transfiguration of our Lord briefly in the Preface, but it is far too rich as a prayer event to stop there. Not only are there lessons to be gained from further reflection, we also need to discover how Jesus's prayer that afternoon makes itself present to the Church today. I invite you to get out your Bible and read Luke 9:28–37. We will then discuss several points from this passage.

JESUS AT PRAYER

Those who were with him were heavy with sleep

Between the transfiguration and the Apostles' sleeping in the Garden of Gethsemane, I spent years wondering whether or not the Apostles suffered from narcolepsy. It wasn't until a few years back that it finally dawned on me that they had just completed a hike up a mountain! To share that awesome moment in Jesus's prayer required effort on their part, and growth in prayer is going to require effort from us, too. That is nothing that should intimidate us. The Apostles did not make that hike by themselves; Jesus was right there beside them, exerting himself; and he's right here with us, too. We actually have a leg up on the Apostles (at least at that point in their lives) because, thanks to our baptism, Jesus is exerting himself from *within us*, pushing us to the next level in prayer. We can do our part by making a commitment to receiving the sacraments regularly, and picking out and beginning to practice faithfully some of the devotions we're studying. Saint Paul had powerful words about our need to cooperate with God's grace (Philem. 2:12–13, 4:13; 1 Cor. 15:10; Heb. 13:20–21).

The appearance of his countenance changed. . . . And a voice came out of the cloud

Here we are reminded of the trinitarian nature of Christian prayer, that it is a sharing in Jesus and the Father's communion in the Spirit. The cloud that "overshadowed" the mountain was the same glory cloud that covered Mt. Sinai in the time of Moses, the *Shekinah.* In Luke's Gospel it is a symbol of the Spirit (Luke 1:35). The voice coming from the cloud is obviously that of the Father. The change in Jesus's face and the way his clothes became "dazzling white" is a revelation of his divinity as Son. Not only does the Spirit proceed from the Father, but also from the Son, illuminating his human heart, mind, and body from within. We want the Holy Spirit to make us transparent to Jesus dwelling within!

Two men talked with him, Moses and Elijah

God the Father spoke to Jesus not just directly through the voice on the mountain, but also through two Old Testament saints. Through Moses and Elijah, the Father spoke with Jesus about his impending "exodus," his crucifixion, resurrection, and ascension. Moses was Israel's lawgiver (who stood behind the first division of the Old Testament canon) and Elijah the greatest of the prophets (the second great division of the Old Testament), so we can be sure it was a very scriptural conversation! What humility on Jesus's part—the Word of the Father allowing his human mind and heart to be spoken to through the very messengers he himself had inspired.

Peter said... "let us make three booths"

Why would Peter want to do that? It seems to indicate that the trans-figuration coincided with the Feast of Tabernacles. It was a week-long feast, so this may be why the gospels made a point of noting how many days elapsed between Peter's confession of faith and the transfiguration ("about eight days" for Luke and six for Matthew and Mark). It would also explain why constructing booths, dwell-ings, would leap to Peter's mind. At Tabernacles, also called the Feast of Booths, Jews commemorated Israel's sojourn in the desert by constructing and living in booths for eight days.

By the time of Jesus, a second meaning had become attached to the booths. They prefigured the new dwellings the righteous would be given when the Messiah appeared. Isaiah had prophesied, "[When] the Spirit is poured upon us from on high ... My people will abide in peaceful habitation, in secure dwellings, and in quiet resting places" (Isa. 32:15,18). The prophet Zechariah also connected this with the time of the Messiah, when even the Gentiles would "go up year after year to worship the King, the LORD of hosts, and to keep the feast of booths" (Zech. 14:16). Zechariah also saw that "liv-ing waters shall flow out from Jerusalem" (14:8). That takes us back to Chapter 2, when Jesus used the water drawing ceremony at another celebration of Tabernacles to teach about the gift of the Spirit: "If any one thirst, let him come to me, and let him who believes in me drink. As the Scripture has said, 'Out of his heart shall flow rivers of living water'" (John 7:37–38).[1]

Reflecting upon Jesus's transfiguration and the Feast of Taberna-cles recently led Pope Benedict to conclude, "[T]he great events of Jesus's life are inwardly connected with the Jewish festival calendar. They are, as it were, liturgical events in which the liturgy, with its remembrance and expectation, becomes reality—becomes life."[2] The Israelites' living in booths in the desert, recalled in the Feast of Tabernacles, receives its fulfillment in Jesus and his Church. "The

---

1. The punctuation of this sentence varies in different biblical manuscripts. For the RSV-CE's justification in using this reading, please consult Timothy O'Donnell, *The Heart of the Redeemer* (San Francisco: Ignatius Press), 44–45.

2. Benedict XVI, *Jesus of Nazareth*, 306–307.

Word became flesh and dwelt [literally "tabernacled"] among us" (John 1:14). He has shared our sojourn through the desert of this world. As we exert ourselves in climbing its crags toward Mt. Zion, the heavenly Jerusalem, our brother Jesus is within us, empowering us to participate in his exodus from this world to the Father. He refreshes us, pouring the living water of the Spirit from his heart to ours, so that with him we can climb the ladder of the Cross and enter the life of heaven.

THE CHURCH AT PRAYER

The Communion of Saints

In the last chapter we saw how Jesus taught us to pray "*Our Father. . . .*" We approach the Father as members of Jesus's mystical body. The transfiguration shows us how Moses and Elijah were drawn into Jesus's communion with the Father, so when you and I invite the saints into our prayer, we are not doing anything novel.

The Father does not feel slighted when we do this, either. The saints in heaven are His *children*! He wants us and them to love and be concerned for one another. We really are in "communion" (from the Latin words *com*—"together"—and *unus*—"union") with one another in Jesus's mystical body. When we draw near to Jesus and the Father, we simultaneously draw near to our brothers and sisters around the throne (Heb. 12:22–24). The saints in heaven constantly surround us, cheering us on to the finish line (Heb. 12:1), and they assist us throughout life by presenting our petitions to God (Rev. 5:8, 8:3–4; see also 6:9–11). As St. Paul wrote, "If one member [of the body] suffers, all suffer together with it; if one member is honored all rejoice together with it" (1 Cor. 12:26).

I have seen the Lord do some amazing things when I have asked the Blessed Mother and St. Therese of Lisieux to pray. Situations that I had prayed about for weeks were resolved in short order after I enlisted their prayers. I know I am not alone in that experience; Christians have been extolling the intercession of the saints for millennia.

Why is it that the Lord sometimes delays his response until we "call in the big guns"? Does he say "no" to us, only to change his mind when the request comes from them? Only a poor theologian would propose something like that! I can't claim to give God's definitive answer, but I put forward a theory in *The God Who Is Love* that I will repeat here:

The Father is building relationships within His family, a family spanning heaven and earth (Eph. 3:15). Our needs give us reasons to reach out to our heavenly brothers and sisters; and when God answers the petitions made in union with them, He establishes and nourishes relationships that will literally last forever. When the Lord responds in this way, it inspires us to learn more about these saints; and God will "speak" to us through their example, analogous to the way He spoke to Jesus through Moses and Elijah,

So get cracking on those novenas to Sts. Joseph, Therese, and Francis. And don't forget to bring our Lady into your prayers—everyone should get to know their mother!

Lectio Divina

Moses and Elijah's appearance to Jesus speaks to us of much more than the communion of saints. They embodied all that the Hebrew Scriptures said to Jesus about his sacrifice, and they remind us how God wants to use Scripture to speak to us, too. Scripture is a *living* Word that God addresses to us here and now with the power to reshape our hearts (Heb. 4:12). When Jesus prayed, the Father spoke to him through the Law (Moses) and the Prophets (Elijah). Throughout the centuries, the Church has sought to share Jesus's experience. It of course does so at Mass, in the Liturgy of the Word, but it urges us, in the strongest terms, to bring Scripture into our daily prayer. (CCC 2653)

Lectio divina, or "divine reading," is a time-honored and simple way of doing just that. In the twelfth century, Guigo, a Carthusian monk, encapsulated it in four simple steps: reading, meditation, (mental) prayer, and contemplation. We will briefly examine each.

Reading seems easy enough to understand. We begin by asking the Holy Spirit to allow us to hear his Word, select a small portion of Scripture, and read it slowly. As we read, we can seek to answer the questions we bring to any piece of literature: Who? What? Where? When? We pay attention to the details the author thought important enough to mention. Perhaps the words chosen by the author allude to earlier passages of the Bible. Our goal is to arrive at what the Church calls the *literal sense* of the passage, or what it objectively means.

Finding the literal sense is much different from taking every word of the Bible *literally*. We Catholics are not fundamentalists, but we do believe everything that the Bible teaches. Confused? The Catholic Church recognizes that the Bible is a *collection* of books, written in the Middle East, thousands of years ago. For the most part, we're going to read stories of people like you and me, following the Lord through times of both tragedy and triumph. But we also encounter different ways of narrating history, symbolic numbers, poetry, apocalyptic literature, and so forth—all operating according to their own set of rules. We need to take that into account to understand what God, and the human author He made use of, really meant to communicate. When people accuse the Bible of containing historical errors or being in conflict with science, it almost always boils down to a misunderstanding of how ancient writers expressed themselves, expecting them to use twentieth-century rules of composition instead of their own.[3] This is why Catholic Bibles are required to have study notes in the margins—so make use of them. Also, don't forget to put your belief in the communion of saints to work for you by asking both the biblical authors and the persons you read about to intercede for you!

Perhaps you are new to reading Scripture and not sure where to begin. Start with the gospels, where you can "hear" and "see" Jesus for yourself. He is the center of Scripture, the One to whom all of the Old Testament pointed, and from whom all of the New Testament flows. Scripture opens his heart to us. (CCC 112) Allow your reading to branch out from the gospels to the Acts of the Apostles

---

3. For a fuller discussion of how Catholics interpret the Bible, I refer you to Chapter 7 of my book *The God Who Is Love: Explaining Christianity from Its Center* (Out of the Box, 2009).

and the epistles, and then begin going through the Old Testament. Come back to the gospels often; they are the meat and potatoes of *lectio divina*.

Meditation is the second stage of *lectio*. In America today, "meditation" usually refers to Eastern spiritualities—legs crossed, back straight, deep breaths, and the *emptying of the mind*. While Christianity has nothing against body positions or breathing, Christian meditation is all about *filling the mind*, focusing it on God and His Word. We invoke the Holy Spirit, asking him to allow us to penetrate what we have read. We want to mull it over again and again, trying to "get inside" of it.

EWTN's Mother Angelica was a master at leading her audience in meditation. Fortunately for us, her programs are still available to us through YouTube and EWTN.[4] Mother said that if you could replay something bad that had been said to you over and over in your head, going at it from every angle, then you already knew how to meditate!

Her meditation on Jesus's multiplication of the loaves and fish in Mark's Gospel serves as an example. She started by asking her audience to imagine the scene as vividly as possible, to put themselves there among the crowd. Then she seized on Mark's detail that the crowd had been with Jesus for three days, so enthralled by what he had said that they did not notice they had skipped meals! Mother asked her viewers to think about that; how enthralled are they with Jesus's teaching? (How enthralled are you and I?)

If you and I looked at Mark's account right now, we could be struck by a completely different element from that which struck Mother Angelica. We might zero in on Mark's choice of words in narrating Jesus's action with the loaves: "took . . . gave thanks . . . broke . . . gave" (Mark 8:6)—the same words Mark used to narrate the institution of the Eucharist (Mark 14:22). Our meditation may explore what the multiplication of the loaves says to us about the ongoing miracle of the Eucharist—how, for example, every particle of the consecrated host contains the whole Christ, allowing him to

4. They can be found online at http://www.ewtn.com/tv/prime/motherangelica.asp.

fill not just our famished hearts, but the hearts of the hundreds who surround us at Sunday Mass.

Prayer, or more precisely mental prayer, is the third element of *lectio*. It flows naturally from our meditation as we begin talking to God dwelling in our hearts about what we have seen. If, like Mother Angelica, our focus was on how absorbed the crowd was by Jesus's message, then we could begin by thanking the Father for the innumerable opportunities we have to hear Jesus teach—in the Bible and Catechism, through the pope and bishops. We might then reflect with the Lord how we make use of those opportunities: Is Scripture a daily part of our relationship with him? Have we ever made a point of reading one of the pope's encyclicals? Ask the Lord, "How can I make your Word a higher priority in my life? What do you want me to do?" Think about it there in the presence of God, exploring options you might pursue. Tell the Lord which one you sense him directing you toward, and ask for the grace to follow through. Then make a resolution to do so.

Many current practitioners of *lectio divina* insert an additional step at this point: *action*. If we fail to translate our prayer and resolutions into concrete actions, then our faith runs the risk of becoming empty words, a head-trip.

The final stage of *lectio divina*, and of all Christian prayer for that matter, is called *contemplation*. It is by far the most difficult to write about. Few souls attain it, and those who do have been hard-pressed to find language to describe it to others. Of those who have made the attempt, the Carmelite saints John of the Cross and Teresa of Avila hold pride of place.

They insist that contemplative prayer is pure gift on God's part, granted to souls that have continually strengthened their "yes" to His will for their lives. The soul no longer strives to form thoughts, to meditate; rather, it is stilled, completely absorbed in God's loving presence dwelling within. The Catechism actually uses Jesus's transfiguration, the very focus of our chapter, in its attempt to explain this kind of prayer. "[It] is a gaze of faith, fixed on Jesus. [T]he light of the countenance of Jesus illumines the eyes of our heart and teaches us to see everything in the light of his truth and compassion for all men." (CCC 2715) It goes on to speak of contemplation as a participation in the prayer of Jesus, a sharing in the "yes" that both he and the Blessed Mother made to the Father. (CCC 2716–19)

As I said, this level of prayer, so exalted above our created natures, remains pure gift on God's part. We are unable to force it any more than we can force the growth of a plant. Our work is to break up the hard soil, see that the seed is planted, and then make sure it remains fed and watered. If St. Jerome was correct that "ignorance of Scripture is ignorance of Christ," and if the Catechism is right when it says that Scripture reveals Christ's heart (CCC 112), then it has to be at the center of our prayer and meditation. The Word of God is the seed (Mark 4:3, 14) and the water (Isa. 55:10–11); and our meditation, prayer, and action are the way we allow it to penetrate and change our souls. We'll never experience the transfiguring power of contemplative prayer until, like the Apostles, we put in the hard work of scaling the mountain *alongside Jesus*. We can't hope for the maturity to accept a gift like contemplation before we've unwrapped and made generous use of the gifts God has already given us, and Scripture is among the highest! (Matt. 25:20–30)

7

Suffering Servant

When the hour had come for him to fulfill the Father's plan of love, Jesus allows a glimpse of the boundless depth of his filial prayer, not only before he freely delivered himself up ("Abba . . . not my will, but yours"), but even in his last words on the Cross, where prayer and the gift of self are but one. . . . ~CCC 2605

A TERMINAL DIAGNOSIS, betrayal, assault, slander—how is one able to pray in the moments following such events? Some of us go numb, while many cry "Why?" in anguish. The gospels give us incredible glimpses into Jesus's heart during the Passion. Both the manner of his death and the few words that escaped his lips reveal an inner world that Christ wants to open to us, too.

At his baptism, the Father addressed Jesus as the suffering servant of Isaiah. In his Passion, the darkest part of Isaiah's prophecy became reality: "it was the will of the LORD to bruise him. [The servant] poured out his soul to death. [H]e bore the sin of many, and made intercession for the transgressors" (Isa. 53:10, 12). When the Father allows tragedy to strike our lives, we participate in Jesus's Passion (Col. 1:24) and, one hopes, his prayer. Throughout the Passion, his prayers were simple, naked expressions of his heart—the bare-boned petitions of the *Our Father* and the psalms he had memorized and prayed since childhood. In his words, but even more so in his actions, he undertook the highest form of prayer—*by making himself a sacrificial gift to the Father.* We'll study his prayer in two stages: in the Garden of Gethsemane and on the Cross; and then in *The Prayer of the Church*, we will explore devotions that seek to take us "inside" the Passion and unite our prayer to those of the Crucified.

JESUS AT PRAYER

Part I: The Garden of Gethsemane

Jesus's path to Gethsemane took him over the small brook that ran through the Kidron Valley (John 18:1). The blood of the Temple sacrifices was emptied into that brook, carried from the Temple by an elaborate drainage system. At Passover time, its water became dark with the blood of tens of thousands of Passover lambs. Jesus had just ended the Passover meal by singing the Hallel (Ps. 115–118); as he stepped over the brook, its words must have reverberated through his mind:

> The snares of death encompassed me; the pangs of Sheol laid hold on me; I suffered distress and anguish.... Oh LORD, I beg you, save my life! ... Precious in the sight of the LORD is the death of his saints. O LORD, I am your servant; I am your servant, the son of your handmaid. (Ps. 116:3–4, 15–16)

> What can mortals do to me? ... The LORD has chastened me sorely, but he has not given me over to death.... The stone which the builders rejected has become the cornerstone. (Ps. 118:6, 18, 22)

The hours Jesus spent in Gethsemane, his agony in the garden, are among the most mysterious in the gospels. God the Son collapsed to the ground and cried through tears, "Abba, Father, all things are possible to you; remove this chalice from me; yet not what I will, but what you will" (Mark 14:35–36; Heb. 5:7). The "sorrow" that pushed him to the point of death (Mark 14:34) was fed by something far more than dread of crucifixion; Jesus encountered the sin of the world in all its gratuity and grotesqueness.

Jesus entered fully into his act of making reparation for our sins. He stepped into the place of sinners, taking, as it were, the weight of our sins upon his shoulders. He witnessed every betrayal, slander, rape, and murder from history's dawn until its end and offered the

Father all the sorrow and contrition that mankind should feel, but does not. He offered the Father the love of which those sins robbed Him.[1]

Jesus's simple words, asking for relief, but much more importantly for the Father's will to be done, made reparation for mankind's disobedience. "The *whole prayer of Jesus* is contained in this loving adherence of his human heart to the mystery of the will of the Father." (CCC 2603; see also Eph. 1:9) "Thy will be done." It was his prayer at the moment of his conception (Heb. 10:5), the prayer of his mother, the Lord's "handmaid" (Ps. 116:16; Luke 1:38), the prayer evoked by the wearing of the *tzitzit* (Num. 15:39), the prayer he gave the Apostles, and us, in the *Our Father*. And Jesus did not cry out "not what I will, but what you will" once, but three times! He learned what it was to cry out for relief and to be met with silence—the Father's "No, not yet."

An angel was sent, but not to whisk him to safety. It came to strengthen him, to allow his body and soul to endure more than humanly possible.[2] The Son who receives all he is from the Father obediently offered himself, through the Spirit, in return, learning what it was to put one foot in front of the other in painful obedience (Heb. 5:8).

Part II: The Cross

In the details they share, the gospel writers direct our eyes to the sacrificial nature of Jesus's death. He went to the Cross wearing a seamless tunic (John 19:24), which was what the high priest wore when offering sacrifice.[3] Jesus was crucified at 9 a.m. (Mark 15:25), the same time the *tamid*—a lamb, bread, and wine—were placed on the

---

1. We share in Jesus's perfect sorrow for sin when we participate in the sacrament of reconciliation. How often do we come to the sacrament with perfect contrition, authentic sorrow for our sins *born from love of God*? Aren't we more often drawn there by fear of hell? Jesus is present in the sacrament, superabundantly compensating for our imperfections. (CCC 1453)

2. Frank Sheed, *To Know Christ Jesus* (San Francisco: Ignatius Press, 1980), 349.

3. Scott Hahn, *The Lamb's Supper: The Mass As Heaven on Earth* (New York: Doubleday, 1999), 23.

altar. He was given a drink via a sponge on a hyssop branch, the same type of branch used to apply the blood of the original Passover lambs to Israelite homes (John 19:29; Exod. 12:22). Also like the Passover lamb, none of Jesus's bones was broken (John 19:36; Exod. 12:46).

Although his crucifixion was one great bodily prayer, there were still moments when Jesus found it necessary to summon his strength and speak. Since inhaling enough air to speak meant pushing his nailed feet against the wood and pulling himself up on the spikes through his wrists, each statement cost Jesus dearly, so their importance cannot be overestimated. We will look at his words to Mary and John and their importance for our prayer lives in Chapter 11. Here our focus is on the words he chose to pray aloud.

Father, forgive them; for they do not know what they are doing.
(Luke 23:34)

At the Sermon on the Mount, Jesus instructed his disciples to "pray for those who persecute you" (Matt. 5:44), and then taught them the words they were to use: "Our Father, . . . forgive us our trespasses, as we forgive those who trespass against us" (Matt. 6:9, 12). Jesus *lived* it.

I know what you are thinking: when you imagine yourself *on his cross*, praying those words seems impossible. But baptism makes it possible! It unites my soul to his. I could never pray those words on my own, apart from the action of the Holy Spirit. But through the Spirit, through the action of grace upon my soul, *Jesus can pray those words in me*; and they can become mine! Each time I pray the *Our Father* and cooperate with his grace to forgive people their small wrongs against me, my soul grows toward forgiving those who would take my life.

My God, my God, why have you forsaken me? (Matt. 27:46)

These words can be troubling without sufficient background knowledge. Some, with a poorly formed understanding of both the Trinity and how Jesus's sacrifice saves us, take these words to mean that Jesus was rejected by the Father. They see salvation purely in terms of Jesus's suffering the punishment due to sinners; Jesus suffered the

Father's wrath—His condemnation and rejection—so that sinners can go free. Catholics recognize that as a woefully inadequate understanding of redemption, not to mention the fact that because God is an eternal *communion*—the Father and Son pouring themselves out to each other in the Spirit—the idea of one member of the Trinity being at odds with another is nonsense, to put it mildly.

Rather, "My God, my God, why have you forsaken me?" was Jesus's praying of the first words of Psalm 22, one of the lamentation psalms he had known since childhood. By crying out its first words, he invoked the psalm in its entirety. (Imagine yourself in great pain, only managing to get out the words "Our Father. . . .") Reading the rest of Psalm 22, it is hard to imagine anyone else being able to pray it as personally as Jesus did:

> All who see me mock me. . . .
> "He committed his cause to the LORD;
> let him deliver him,
> let him rescue him, for he delights in him!"
> . . . My heart is like wax,
> it is melted within my breast. . . .
> a company of evildoers encircle me;
> they have pierced my hands and feet—
> I can count all my bones—
> they stare and gloat over me;
> they divide my garments among them;
> and for my clothing they cast lots.
> But you, O LORD, be not far off!
> O my help, hasten to my aid!
> (Ps. 22:7–8, 14, 16–19)

Not only did it mirror his physical suffering exactly, it also mirrored the spiritual suffering he underwent since Gethsemane ("my heart . . . melts within me," i.e., dies). Jesus was never abandoned by his Father, but his human soul "saw" sin in all its putridness and was desolated by it. Despite that, the Catechism says he loved and clasped us sinners to himself so tightly on the Cross that he was praying in *our name* when he cried, "why have you forsaken me?" (CCC 603)

Like many of the lamentation psalms, Psalm 22 shifts from suffering to joyful praise, *berakah*, as either God intervenes, or the sufferer anticipates God's intervention on his behalf.

> I will tell of your name to my brethren;
> in the midst of the congregation I will praise you. . . .
> From you comes my praise in the great congregation;
> my vows I will pay before those who fear him.
> The poor shall eat and be satisfied;
> those who seek him shall praise the LORD!
> May your hearts live forever!
> (Ps. 22:22, 25–26)

The "poor shall eat and be satisfied" refers to the *todah* sacrifice celebrated in thanksgiving (*eucharistia* in Greek) for God saving a life. If you recall from Chapter 2, part of the victim was offered to God by fire and the other portion eaten in a sacred meal by the offerer and those dear to him. Prayed by Jesus, it referred to the Eucharist, the sacrificial meal of the New Covenant that truly enables our hearts to "enjoy life forever."

Jesus even used Psalm 22 to praise the Father for the way salvation would reach beyond Israel to the Gentiles, and both backward (to the dead) and forward to future generations:

> All the ends of the earth shall remember and turn to the LORD;
> And all the families of the nations shall worship before him. . . .
> [B]efore him shall bow all who go down to the dust,
> and he who cannot keep himself alive.
> Posterity shall serve him;
> men shall tell of the Lord to the coming generation,
> and proclaim his deliverance to a people yet unborn,
> that he has wrought it.
> (Ps. 22:27, 29–31)

All of this was contained in Jesus's "My God, my God. . . ." The epistle to the Hebrews seems to capture Jesus's motivation in praying Psalm 22: "for the joy that was set before him [he] endured the cross, despising the shame" (Heb. 12:2). We need to pray Psalm 22 when difficulties hit, to envision ourselves merged with Jesus on the Cross—*because we are*—and use its words to express our pain honestly to God as well as to praise Him, in faith and hope, for the amazing future He has promised us.

Jesus said (to fulfill the Scripture), "I thirst." (John 19:28)

One of the bystanders understood it as the request of a dying man and lifted a vinegar-soaked sponge to Jesus's lips—so why am I treating it as a prayer? Because the Scripture that was fulfilled ("For my thirst they gave me vinegar to drink") is from Psalm 69, another lamentation psalm. If Jesus spoke those words to "fulfill" the psalm, then I feel secure in believing that he also prayed it:

> I am weary with my crying;
> my throat is parched.
> My eyes grow dim
> with waiting for my God. . . .
> For it is for your sake that I have borne reproach,
> that shame has covered my face. . . .
> For zeal for your house has consumed me,
> and the insults of those who insult you have fallen on me. . . .
> Let not the flood sweep over me,
> or the deep swallow me up,
> or the pit close its mouth over me. . . .
> Insults have broken my heart,
> so that I am in despair. . . .
> They gave me gall for food,
> and for my thirst they gave me vinegar to drink.
> (Ps. 69:3, 7, 9, 15, 20–21)

This psalm also turns from lament and petition to *berakah* for the deliverance God will ultimately bring:

> I will praise the name of God with a song;
> I will magnify him with *thanksgiving* [or *todah*].
> This will please the Lord more than an ox
> or a bull with horns and hoofs.
> Let the humble see it and be glad;
> you who seek God, *let your hearts revive*.
> (Ps. 69:30–31)

I believe that Jesus used this psalm to praise the Father for the way that the resurrection of his broken heart (69:20) would lead to the revival, the transformation, of our sinful hearts (69:32). And this transformation is tied to Jesus's thanksgiving sacrifice (again,

79

eucharistia in Greek) that will fulfill and go beyond the Temple sacrifices. When you and I suffer, let us make a point of reaching out to Jesus in the Eucharist for the strength our hearts need to persevere.

Father, into your hands I commit my spirit! (Luke 23:46)

Once again, Jesus expresses himself through a psalm, one that moves from lament to the effect that the deliverance God gives him will have on the hearts of others.

> Into your hand I commit my spirit;
> you have redeemed me, O LORD,
> faithful God. . . .
> Yes, I hear the whispering of many—terror on every side!—
> as they scheme together against me,
> as they plot to take my life. . . .
> Blessed be the LORD,
> for he has wondrously shown me his merciful love
> when I was beset as in a besieged city. . . .
> Love the LORD, all you his saints! . . .
> Be strong, and let your heart take courage,
> all you who wait for the LORD!
> (Ps. 31:5, 13, 21, 23–24)

When Jesus suffered, he relied on the prayers he had known since childhood—"rote" prayers. With his soul devastated by the sin of the world and his flesh hanging from him like rags, the words that had been ingrained in his mind through years of repetition became his means for pouring his heart out to the Father. And they weren't empty words; they captured what the Lord was going through. The Church's traditional prayers—the *Our Father, Hail Mary,* the Psalms, etc.—are meant to do the same for us!

And Jesus cried again with a loud voice and yielded up his spirit. (Matt. 27:50)

It was as if Jesus gathered up all the life he had left and poured it out to the Father in one final torrent. Through his broken body he showed the eternal gift, the eternal communication, he makes of himself to the Father, in the Holy Spirit (Heb. 9:14)—and made reparation for all humanity's refusals to love. On the Cross, where prayer and the gift of self were one and the same, Jesus's final cry drew into itself every petition and intercession humanity had ever, or would ever, make. (CCC 2605–06)

The Catechism's insight is a keen one. Jesus culminated his sacrifice and prayer at the same time the evening *tamid* was being offered in the Temple, and at the same time that Jews throughout the Middle East joined themselves to it by praying the Eighteen Benedictions: "Blessed be the Lord . . . who raises the dead. . . . Forgive us our sins against you. . . . Heal the pain in our hearts. [R]estore the Kingdom of David. . . . Blessed be the Lord who hears our prayers. . . ." Jesus was the answer to their petitions. His death, resurrection, and ascension fulfilled the *tamid*, the Passover—all the sacrifices of the Law! When Jesus died, the Temple service was disrupted as the curtain that separated the Holy of Holies was torn in two, from top to bottom (Mark 15:38). Jesus's sacrifice—the tearing of his flesh—opened a way for us into the depths of the Trinity (Heb. 10:19)!

Because of Jesus, when we face trials we can to go to God as our Father and spiritually throw ourselves into his arms. When we are so distraught that our minds cannot form the words of even the *Our Father*, then we can share in Jesus's final prayer, his cry, knowing that "the Spirit himself intercedes for us with sighs too deep for words. And he who searches the hearts of men knows what is the mind of the Spirit" (Rom. 8:26–27).

[O]ne of the soldiers pierced his side with a spear, and at once there came out blood and water. [T]hese things took place that the scripture might be fulfilled. . . . "They shall look on him whom they have pierced." (John 19:34, 37)

The Scripture John quotes is from Zechariah, and it continues, "On that day there shall be a fountain opened for the house of David and the inhabitants of Jerusalem to cleanse them from sin and uncleanness" (Zech. 13:1). The water and blood that issued from Jesus's pierced side, his pierced heart, is a graphic witness to the effect of his sacrificial death: The Holy Spirit would be poured out on humanity through the water of baptism and his Eucharistic blood! (1 John 5:7–8; 1 Cor. 12:13) This was what Jesus spoke of at the water-drawing ceremony on the Feast of Tabernacles, when he promised the thirsty crowd that living water would flow from his heart (John 7:37–38). John explained, "this [Jesus] said about the Spirit, which those who believed in him were to receive; for as yet the Spirit had not been given, because Jesus was not yet glorified [on the Cross]" (John 7:39). Pentecost began at the Cross!

THE CHURCH AT PRAYER

There are several ways we can enter into the prayer of Jesus's Passion. Sacramentally, we do so in the Eucharist, which we will explore separately in Chapter 9. Here we want to look at devotions such as the Stations of the Cross, the solemn intercessions of Good Friday, the Divine Mercy devotion, and prayers and acts of reparation. First, however, we should look at an experience common to all of us.

When God Says "No"

God is a Father, and—as you have surely discovered by experience—a Father who sometimes answers our petitions with "No." It happened to Jesus in the Garden of Gethsemane. Well, that isn't completely accurate, though, is it? Yes, Jesus begged the Father to remove the cup of suffering, *but only if that was what the Father willed*. No matter how strongly Jesus's human emotions may have cried out for relief, his ultimate desire, the deepest prayer of his human heart, was always for the Father's will to be accomplished. Our core attitude needs to be the same—and like the Lord, we may need to wait for an angel (an infusion of grace) to bring calm to the surface.

God's will is mysterious, to be sure; but since I became a dad, I'm a little more at peace with that. My children ask for, or ask my permission to do, so many things that are dangerous to them—at least, while they're small. They of course disagree; they think there is no way the tree branch they want to stand on, twenty feet up, will break, and they definitely don't believe me when I say that seventy degrees is too cold to go to the pool! Parents make decisions with a much wider knowledge base than their children.

The challenge is for children to remember that these decisions are always made out of love and a sincere desire for their well-being. I wish my daughter could have understood that when she was a year old and I had to hold her still, despite her screams, so the doctor could administer a second immunization shot; but it was completely beyond her comprehension. When God says "No" to our pleading, we need to exercise the *gift* of faith to believe He acts with love and ultimately in our best interests.

As that gift of faith matures, we begin thinking about our lives with an eye to eternity and evaluating life's highs and lows in terms of the effect they have on our souls. Do these things bring out the image of Jesus, or obscure it? Allow me to give another personal example—my divorce.

It was something I never wanted. When my wife told me that she had been considering it for some months, I begged her to reconsider. I prayed like mad. I understood that God respected her free will, but He's the same God that knocked Saul off his horse and turned him into the apostle Paul. He surely could have changed my wife's heart; but He allowed her to go down that road. Bottom line—I did not want to be divorced, but I am.

What amazed me about the whole thing was how I reacted to it. I have always struggled with forgiveness; and yet I found myself continuing to desire good for my spouse and feeling compassion for her. I made a conscious act to put the future in God's hands and saw financial difficulties and housing questions work out better than I could have ever dreamed. I took stock of myself during my married years and think I've become much more patient and a more responsible and grateful steward of the gifts God has entrusted to me. As an example, I'm in better physical health now than at any time in the past fifteen years; and here I am having more opportunities to share about our Faith than ever before. Yes, there is still healing from the divorce to be done; but I know from experience that "in everything God works for good with those who love him, who are called according to his purpose" (Rom. 8:28).

Things could have gone differently. I could have lashed out in bitterness. I could have countered the rejection by seeking out an illicit relationship, or drowned my sorrows in a bottle. And quite honestly, "there but for the grace of God. . . ." I am under no illusions as to my own strength. What I did do was identify with Jesus in his Passion, and I prayed the *Our Father* from the heart, just as he did then: "Thy kingdom come, *thy will be done*. . . . Forgive us our trespasses *as we forgive those who trespass against us*, and lead us not into *temptation*." If we endure the pain of the present moment with Jesus, in loving obedience, then we'll eventually experience his resurrection (Rom. 8:17)—and it is worth the wait!

The Stations of the Cross

This devotion, also called the Way of the Cross, goes back to the early centuries of the Church. Egeria, a third-century pilgrim from Spain to the Holy Land, recorded how people gathered with the bishop late Holy Thursday in the Garden of Gethsemane, and how over the next several hours processed from there, through Jerusalem, to the Church of the Holy Sepulcher, built over the site of Jesus's crucifixion and tomb.

Over time, specific places came to be identified with episodes in Jesus's carrying of the Cross: meeting Simon of Cyrene, the women mourning, etc. The Franciscans, to whom guardianship of the holy places was entrusted in 1342, fostered the devotion of tracing Jesus's journey to Golgotha. The number of stations varied depending on which friar led the group, but the path quickly became known as the *Via Dolorosa*, or Sorrowful Way.

Because many Europeans couldn't hope to make a pilgrimage to the Holy Land, the *Via Dolorosa* was recreated on the grounds of European monasteries and convents. Some religious orders sent members to measure the exact distance between stations! Artistic representations of the events were then painted or chiseled as an aid to the faithful. In 1731, Pope Clement XII extended an indulgence to those who made a Way of the Cross consisting of fourteen stations, and from that point on fourteen has been their number. Clement's successor, Benedict XIV, encouraged all priests to have the stations erected in their parishes. We see the success of his efforts whenever we attend Mass.

Making the Way of the Cross is a means for us to meditate on

Jesus's Passion. Ideally we should bring our own "crosses" to the devotion and unite our difficulties to Jesus's hardships. At each point in his journey there is a lesson for us, some element to which we can connect our lives. The fourteen traditional stations are:

1. Jesus is condemned to death.
2. He receives the Cross.
3. He falls the first time.
4. He meets his Mother.
5. Simon of Cyrene helps carry the Cross.
6. Veronica wipes his face.
7. He falls the second time.
8. He meets the mourning women.
9. He falls the third time.
10. He is stripped of his garments.
11. He is nailed to the Cross.
12. He dies.
13. He is taken down from the Cross.
14. He is laid in the tomb.

At the beginning of each, it is traditional to pray, "We adore thee O Christ and we bless thee, because by thy holy Cross thou hast redeemed the world." We then make an effort to visualize the station as best we can, to place ourselves within our Lord's body and heart, or within the heart of the Blessed Mother watching these events. It is common to finish the meditation with the *Our Father*, *Hail Mary*, and *Glory Be*.

Those familiar with Scripture will of course wonder about the inclusion of events not narrated therein: three falls, Jesus meeting his mother, Veronica wiping his face. The first two points are merely matters of deduction: To require Simon of Cyrene's help carrying the Cross, Jesus had to be in a weakened condition, and undoubtedly suffered falls. John's Gospel tells us that the Blessed Mother was at the foot of the Cross. Wouldn't she and Jesus have exchanged words, or at least have locked eyes, at some point during his carrying of the Cross? Veronica's wiping Jesus's face, however, does not appear in the written record until the third century. While it could be historical, a surviving unwritten tradition, I tend to view it as naturally flowing from Christians' love for our Lord—our desire to give him some measure of relief during his way of sorrow.

You are certainly free to develop your own stations of the cross, too. In 1991 and 1994, John Paul II departed from the traditional fourteen. His stations began with the agony in the garden and included meditations such as Peter's denial and Jesus's words to Mary and John. What if we followed John Paul's lead and incorporated each of Jesus's prayers from the Cross into our praying of the stations?

Good Friday's Solemn Intercessions

Once a year in the Liturgy of the Lord's Passion, after listening to John's account of Jesus's death, the Church offers a series of petitions. They are reminiscent of the Eighteen Benedictions that were prayed as Jesus completed his sacrifice. They give voice to the prayer of Jesus's heart, asking the Father's blessing upon:

1. The Church

2. The Pope

3. All of the faithful

4. Catechumens (those preparing for baptism)

5. The unity of Christians

6. The Jewish people

7. Those who do not believe in Christ

8. Atheists

9. Those who hold public office

10. Those suffering tribulation

86

Suffering Servant

The Divine Mercy Devotion

Faustina Kowalska, a Polish nun, entered eternal life in 1938, at the age of thirty-three. In her thirteen years as a nun, however, the Lord communicated to her a devotion, uniting our petitions—particularly those for God's mercy—to his offering upon the Cross. The devotion consists of several elements, any of which can enrich our prayer lives: the Divine Mercy image, the chaplet of Divine Mercy, prayer during the hour of mercy (3 PM), the Feast of Divine Mercy, and the novena preceding it.

On February 22, 1931, Faustina saw an apparition of our Lord. He was clothed in a white garment, one hand raised in blessing, and the other slightly parting the garment at his chest. Two large rays, one red and the other pale, emanated from his heart. The Lord directed her to "[p]aint an image according to the pattern you see, with the signature, 'Jesus, I trust in You.' I desire that this image be venerated . . . throughout the world."[4] When asked to explain the image, our Lord responded, "The two rays denote Blood and Water. The pale ray stands for the Water which makes souls righteous. The red ray stands for the Blood which is the life of souls. . . . These two rays issued from the very depths of My tender mercy when My agonized Heart was opened by a lance on the Cross."[5]

"Jesus, I *trust* in You." Trust, the absolute conviction that Jesus's heart is filled with mercy for us, is a striking feature of the devotion. Faustina reported the Lord saying, "The graces of my mercy are drawn by means of one vessel only, and that is—trust. The more a soul trusts, the more it will receive. . . . I am sad when souls ask for little, when they narrow their hearts."[6]

To implore God's mercy, Jesus imparted a prayer to Faustina. It has become known as the chaplet of Divine Mercy:

First of all, you will say one *Our Father* and *Hail Mary* and the *I Believe in God*. Then on the *Our Father* beads you will say the

4. Mary Faustina Kowalska, *Diary: Divine Mercy in My Soul* (Stockbridge, MA: Marians of the Immaculate Conception, 1996), no. 47.
5. Ibid., no. 299.
6. Ibid., no. 1578.

following words: "Eternal Father, I offer You the Body and Blood, Soul and Divinity of Your dearly beloved Son, Our Lord Jesus Christ, in atonement for our sins and those of the whole world." On the *Hail Mary* beads you will say the following words: "For the sake of His sorrowful Passion have mercy on us and on the whole world." In conclusion, three times you will recite these words: "Holy God, Holy Might One, Holy Immortal One, have mercy on us and on the whole world."[7]

The chaplet recalls the great truths that we are a priestly people (1 Pet. 2:9) and that Jesus's sacrifice is the most precious offering we can bring before the Father, the reason for all the grace that flows to us. With this central truth in mind, we listen to the promise made to Faustina: "My daughter, encourage souls to say the chaplet which I have given to you. It pleases Me to grant everything they ask of Me by saying the chaplet. When hardened sinners say it, I will fill their souls with peace, and the hour of their death will be a happy one."[8]

Jesus further instructed Faustina to immerse herself in prayer for his mercy from 3–4 PM daily—the hour of his death and the *tamid*:

Invoke [My mercy's] omnipotence for the whole world, and particularly for poor sinners. [I]t was the hour of grace for the whole world. [T]ry your best to make the stations of the Cross in this hour … and if you are not able … immerse yourself in prayer there where you happen to be, if only for a brief instant.[9]

Jesus also told Faustina that he wanted the Sunday following Easter to be a celebration of Divine Mercy. He promised, "The soul that will go to Confession and receives Holy Communion [on that day] shall obtain complete forgiveness of sins and punishment."[10] In preparation, he requested that Faustina make a yearly novena, nine days of prayer to begin on Good Friday and finish on the Saturday before the feast. "On each day you will bring to My Heart a different

---

7. Ibid., no. 476.
8. Ibid., no. 1541.
9. Ibid., no. 1572.
10. Ibid., no. 699.

group of souls, and you will immerse them in this ocean of My mercy":[11]

1. All humanity, especially sinners

2. Priests and religious

3. Devout and faithful souls

4. Non-Christians and atheists

5. Christians not united to the Church

6. The meek and humble, and children

7. Those who glorify and love Jesus's mercy

8. Souls in purgatory

9. Those who are lukewarm

Like the Solemn Intercessions of Good Friday, these intentions invite us to participate in Jesus's intercession.

As a matter of private revelation the Church can never make the Divine Mercy devotion incumbent on her people. I doubt anyone reading this, however, would dispute it as a singular way to enter into the intercession Jesus made through his Passion. Blessed John Paul II was devoted to it. In the year 2000 he invited the entire Church to turn anew to God's mercy by establishing the Second Sunday of the Easter season as Divine Mercy Sunday and attaching a plenary indulgence to its celebration—but more on that in the next chapter.

Offering Reparation for Sin

Jesus received baptism, a baptism of *repentance*, as our representative. Jesus redeemed us by giving the Father the loving obedience we had denied Him. In the desert, he withstood temptations to which Adam and Israel had succumbed. Jesus lived his identity as Son even when it meant being scourged, crowned with thorns, nailed to a tree, and pierced with a spear. By saying "yes" and enduring it all

11. Ibid., no. 1209. The intentions for each of the nine days are discussed in detail in nos. 1210–30.

in obedience to God's will, Jesus redeemed the "no" of our sins. Let me be absolutely clear: The eternal punishment of sin, the separation from God that we call Hell, he atoned for—totally, completely, even *super*abundantly. Having said that, we Catholics also believe that, *joined to Jesus*, we are called to offer satisfaction, or *reparation*, for sins committed after being joined to Christ in baptism—both our own and those of other members of the mystical body. I'll do my best to explain why this is.

From time to time you hear of a "jailhouse conversion." Someone was baptized in infancy but received no real formation in the Faith, and goes from one bad decision in life to another. He finally murders someone and is jailed. While in jail he experiences a profound conversion. He understands he has done something incredibly evil and vows to live a new life. The visiting priest hears his confession and gives him absolution. The convict's sins are really and truly forgiven. Jesus's sacrificial death (pure love) atoned for the act of murder (hate) and reconciled the prisoner's soul to God, saving him from hell. Since the prisoner has been forgiven in this way, shouldn't he be released? Something tells me that I am not the only one saying "no."

We understand that even though Jesus's death has atoned for the *eternal* punishment of his sins and that heaven now stands open to the man, there is still an earthly penalty to be paid here in time and space. It's called the *temporal* punishment of sin; and it's not just the state requiring this of the man, either, but God.

Analogously, this is why the Church insists that even though we've been absolved of our sins in the sacrament of reconciliation, we need to perform an act of penance. Penance is a concrete act meant to repair or, when that is impossible, to make amends for the harm we have done and get us walking in the right direction again. (You no doubt remember how Peter, who denied the Lord three times, was asked by the risen Jesus to reaffirm his love three times.)

Note that the Church is saying this to baptized Christians, members of Christ's mystical body. A state board of corrections will not recognize it, but the Church understands that baptism wipes away eternal punishment, *as well as all temporal punishment they have earned*, up until that point. The baptized soul has been regenerated by grace and made a child of God. As a "newborn" it is completely free of all punishment!

But when a Christian sins *after* baptism, when she acts out of selfishness instead of love, then her loving Father disciplines her. "Every one to whom much is given, of him will much be required" (Luke 12:48). Do not be discouraged by this. "My son, do not regard lightly the discipline of the Lord, nor lose courage when you are punished by him. . . . God is treating you as sons; for what son is there whom his father does not discipline?" (Heb. 12:5, 7). And you're not going through this discipline by yourself—you're filled with the strength of Christ (Phil. 4:13). Jesus's love of the Father is so superabundant that it erupts into acts of love in our own lives, acts that make satisfaction for our sins. "I am the vine, you are the branches. He who abides in me, and I in him, he it is that *bears much fruit*" (John 15:5). The branches produce fruit because of the sap they receive from the vine, and we produce acts of love because of the Holy Spirit we receive from Jesus.

We also can't forget that the Christian life isn't just "me and Jesus." He isn't at work just in us, but in the whole communion of saints! In the body of Christ, "If one member suffers, all suffer together" (1 Cor. 12:26). That is why St. Paul went on to say, "Now I rejoice in my sufferings for your sake, and in my flesh I complete what is lacking in Christ's afflictions for the sake of his body, that is, the Church" (Col. 1:24). United to Jesus and empowered by his grace, Paul could make reparation for the sins—the failures to love—of other members of the body.

We can consciously choose to enter into this great act of making reparation. We ask Jesus to fill us with strength and allow us to express his love for the Father, in reparation both for our failings and those of his whole body. We can perform the spiritual and corporal works of mercy (see Chapter 5). Maybe we tighten our belts, literally through fasting or figuratively by almsgiving.[12] Like St. Paul we can be embracing and offering up the frustrations and sufferings God allows to come our way. Reparation can be performing a kind

---

12. "As water extinguishes a blazing fire, so almsgiving atones for sin" (Sir. 3:30).

act, additional Mass attendance during the week, or asking the Lord to forgive another person's sins.[13] Any element of the Divine Mercy is an incredible prayer of reparation! All of this springs from the same love, the same Holy Spirit that Jesus poured forth on the Cross.

Almost everyone has heard the story of Fatima, how the Blessed Mother appeared to three shepherd children in Portugal during World War I. Europe was experiencing the natural result, or the "temporal punishment," of abandoning its love of God and neighbor. Mary came to request a return to the Gospel and reparation for sin through the praying of the Rosary and acts of penance. What many are unaware of was how the children were prepared for Mary's visitation, over a year before, through the appearance of an angel. Teaching the children to prostrate themselves with their foreheads to the ground, he instructed them to pray three times, "My God, I believe, I adore, I hope, and I love You! I ask pardon of You for those who do not believe, do not adore, do not hope, and do not love You."[14]

Pope Pius XI, who became pope shortly after the events at Fatima, made a profound connection between our prayers and acts of reparation and Jesus's Passion. In his encyclical *On Reparation to the Sacred Heart*, he speculated that the angel who "strengthened" Jesus in the Garden of Gethsemane (Luke 22:43) crossed time and space to bring him *our acts of reparation*!

13. "If you see your brother or sister committing what is not a mortal sin, you will ask, and God will give life to such a one—to those whose sin is not mortal" (1 John 5:16).

14. Sister Lucia, *"Calls" from the Message of Fatima* (Still River, MA: Ravengate Press, 2005), 60.

8

Risen, Heavenly High Priest

Believers already truly participate in the heavenly life of the risen Christ, but this life remains "hidden with Christ in God." ⟶Col. 3:3; CCC 1003

As "high priest of the good things to come" [Jesus] is the center and principal actor of the liturgy that honors the Father in heaven. ⟶Heb. 9:11; Rev. 4:6–11; CCC 662

ON THE CROSS we saw Jesus fuse "prayer" with the offering of his life to the Father (CCC 2605), and in this chapter we will see how that continued through his resurrection and ascension. This chapter is of course different from those that have preceded it. We continue to look at our Lord's prayer, but it is the prayer of the *resurrected* Jesus. He remains a man, but one able to function and "pray" in a manner far beyond you and me. And yet Scripture provides us inroads, tries to lift the veil on Jesus's life in glory, the priesthood he exercises in heaven. It even goes so far as to claim that you and I already mystically participate in it.

JESUS AT PRAYER

The Power of the Resurrection

The actual moment of the resurrection is hidden from our eyes—a moment of intimacy reserved to Father, Son, and Spirit. Inseparable from the Cross, it forms one grand trinitarian movement. When Jesus surrendered his human life to the Father completely and irrevocably upon the Cross, the Father responded in turn. Through the Spirit, the Father poured Himself out to the Son; *through the Spirit* He raised Jesus from the dead (Rom. 1:4; Eph. 1:19–20). In a way beyond our comprehension, Jesus's very body was brought into the trinitarian life. (CCC 648) The deliverance he prayed for in Gethsemane and on the Cross arrived! (Heb. 5:7–9)

His humanity has taken on the glory glimpsed at the transfiguration. Prayer is no longer an activity that he must make time for, away from the crowds. He *is prayer*—in his humanity, as he has always been in his divinity. He is spiritually *and bodily* united to the Father in an "indestructible life" (Heb. 7:16). And we participate in it through the Spirit given us at baptism when we were made "partakers of the divine nature" (2 Pet. 1:4).

The Lesson of Emmaus

During the forty days between Jesus's resurrection and ascension, there must have been times when he prayed with the Apostles. From the small amount we are told of that period, I want to suggest that they celebrated the Eucharist; and I will explain why.

Jesus prayed Psalms 22 and 69 on the Cross, both of which look forward to celebrating a thanksgiving sacrifice (*todah* in Hebrew and *eucharistia* in Greek) after being delivered from death. Recall how in a *todah* sacrifice only a part of the sacrificial victim was placed on the altar, with the rest being consumed by the offerer, his family, and friends in a sacred meal. It expressed "communion with God, in whose sacrifice people are permitted to share, and communion among participants" and always began with *berakah* over bread and wine.[1]

Jesus made provision for the celebration of his *todah* at the Last Supper. Jesus "took bread, and when he had given thanks, he broke it and gave it to them, saying, 'This is my body which is given for you. Do this in remembrance of me.' And *likewise the chalice* after supper, saying, 'This chalice which is poured out for you is the new covenant in my blood'" (Luke 22:19–20).

---

1. Joseph Ratzinger, *The Feast of Faith* (San Francisco: Ignatius Press, 1986), 53.

Now, what did Jesus do on Easter Sunday, even before appearing to the Apostles? He approached two downcast disciples, traveling the road from Jerusalem to Emmaus. Concealing his identity, he joined their conversation about what had just transpired. "Was it not necessary that the Messiah should suffer these things and enter into his glory? And beginning with Moses and all the prophets, he interpreted to them in all the Scriptures the things concerning himself" (Luke 24:26–27). Jesus was building toward the crescendo. "When he was at table with them, he took the bread and blessed and broke it, and gave it to them. *And their eyes were opened and they recognized him*; and he vanished out of their sight" (Luke 24:30–31). Jesus celebrated Mass with them—the Liturgy of the Word and Liturgy of the Eucharist! Notice how Luke used the same four verbs here as at the Last Supper (took, blessed, broke, gave). The risen Messiah celebrated his *todah*! If Jesus couldn't hold off celebrating Mass until he appeared to the Apostles a few hours later, then how many times do you think he celebrated it *with them* over those next forty days? Amazingly the Jewish *Talmud* records the ancient teaching that in the Messianic age all sacrifices would cease—all, that is, except the *todah*; it would be celebrated for all eternity.[2]

Ascension / Ministry in the Heavenly Temple

The trinitarian circle of self-offering is endless. Jesus gave himself on the Cross, received himself anew in the resurrection, only to give himself to the Father again in the ascension. Now at the Father's "right hand," he acts as our heavenly high priest.

Jesus actually exhibited his priesthood in the very act of ascending. In Chapter 2 we learned how the *tamid* was concluded. The priests stood on the steps of the Holy Place, with their hands raised, and intoned a blessing over the people. We find a parallel at the conclusion of Luke's Gospel. "Then [Jesus] led them out as far as Bethany, and lifting up his hands he blessed them. While he blessed them, he parted from them, and was carried up into heaven" (Luke

---

2. Scott Hahn, *The Lamb's Supper* (New York: Doubleday, 1999), 33.

24:50–51).[3] Jesus blessed them as he ascended the "steps" of the true Holy Place, Heaven. We are seriously mistaken if we think Jesus's ministry ended in Palestine. His resurrection and ascension brought him to the very height of it!

On the day of Pentecost, Peter told his Jewish compatriots that Jesus's ascension was foretold in Psalm 110, and quoted the first verse. "The LORD said to my lord: 'Sit at my right hand, till I make your enemies your footstool" (Ps. 110:1; Acts 2:33–35). That psalm went on to speak of Christ's priesthood: "The LORD has sworn and will not change his mind, 'You are a priest forever according to the order of Melchizedek'" (Ps. 110:4). If you are unfamiliar with Melchizedek, do not feel bad—the book of Genesis only devoted three verses to him. We need to look at them, though, to understand Jesus's priesthood.

Melchizedek was the king-priest of Salem (later renamed Jerusalem). He met the patriarch Abraham as the latter was returning from a military victory. Melchizedek offered a thanksgiving sacrifice on Abraham's behalf—*bread and wine*—with the prayer, "Blessed be Abram by God Most High, maker of heaven and earth; and blessed be God Most High, who has delivered your enemies into your hand!" (Gen. 14:19–20). He offered bread and wine in *todah*, acting as a prophetic image of Jesus, who makes his sacrifice present *under the appearance of* bread and wine!

What is Jesus *doing* in heaven? He intercedes for the Church on earth by eternally offering himself to the Father, in the Spirit, through the glorious wounds of his Passion (Heb. 7:25, 9:14; Rev. 5:6–14). United to him by baptism, we are spiritually already with him in the presence of the Father (Eph. 2:6). As members of his body, we participate in his priesthood, with all our petitions, praise, thanksgiving, and sacrifices being offered to the Father through him. The prayer of the body is that of the head—and, one hopes, vice versa.

The book of Revelation uses vivid images to describe the liturgy of heaven. Jesus is shown as a Lamb, slain yet alive. As powerful

---

3. Jesus's blessing was efficacious; we see the graces it called down upon the Church at work throughout the book of Acts.

angels worship, saints prostrate themselves and "cast their crowns" before the Father's throne, making a return to Him of the life and graces He gave them (Rev. 4:10). Saints and angels sing their adoration and thanksgiving in rounds as they offer "incense" to the Lord—the prayers of His people on earth (Rev. 5:8, 8:3–4). The worship of heaven is manifested and *participated in* by us on earth when we celebrate the Eucharist, the subject of our next chapter.

THE CHURCH AT PRAYER

We first need to investigate how Divine Mercy Sunday and the sacraments of healing (CCC 1421) give us a share in Jesus's resurrection.

Divine Mercy Sunday

Did you realize that the Feast of the Lord's resurrection is so great that eight of our calendar days are folded into one great liturgical day? That's right—we celebrate the *Octave* of Easter. To help us understand the significance, Blessed John Paul II declared that the Second Sunday of Easter would be known throughout the Church as Divine Mercy Sunday.

When he did so at the canonization Mass of St. Mary Faustina Kowalska, he called the Church to listen to the Scripture readings for the Second Sunday of Easter. He pointed out how Psalm 118 seemed to come to the Church from the Jesus's very lips: "O give thanks to the LORD for he is good; his mercy endures forever" (Ps. 118:1). In the Gospel, the resurrected Christ appears to the Apostles, with the proofs of God's love for them—especially the wound in his heart—still on his body; and he dispatches them to bring God's love and mercy to the world. "As the Father has sent me, even so I send you. . . . Receive the Holy Spirit. If you forgive the sins of any, they are forgiven; if you retain the sins of any, they are retained" (John 20:21–23).[4]

---

4. See Bd. John Paul II, *Homily for The Canonization of Sr. Mary Faustina Kowalska,* April 30, 2000. http://www.va/holy_father/john_paul_ii/homilies/documents/hf_jp-ii_hom_20000430_faustina_en.html.

As an incentive for the faithful's special celebration of the day, John Paul also made it an opportunity for gaining a plenary indulgence, a complete remission of the temporal punishment of sin. He explained his reason for doing so: that having experienced God's mercy and the gift of the Holy Spirit, we are moved to forgive those who sin against us. To obtain the indulgence, a person must (a) take part in the prayers and devotions held in honor of Divine Mercy, or (b) "recite the *Our Father* and the Creed, adding a devout prayer to the merciful Lord Jesus (such as 'Merciful Jesus, I trust in you!')." These are in addition to the usual requirements for receiving an indulgence: sacramental confession, detachment from affection for even venial sin, receiving the Eucharist, and praying for the intentions of the pope. Divine Mercy Sunday is now one of the Church's great treasures, an opportunity for all of us to appropriate the graces won by our Lord's Passover. The impetus for John Paul to bring it about may have been the Divine Mercy devotion (studied in Chapter 7); but tied as it is to the heart of the Gospel, it is an unassailable development in the Church's liturgical year.

The Sacrament of Reconciliation

The Gospel reading for Divine Mercy Sunday tells us that Jesus chose Easter to institute the sacrament of reconciliation. "If you forgive the sins of any they are forgiven. . . ." (John 20:23). The Lord knew that most of us would fall into mortal sin at some point, cutting ourselves off again from the Father; and he made provisions. When we fall, we shouldn't despair. "For we have not a high priest who is unable to sympathize with our weaknesses, but one who in every respect has been tempted as we are, yet without sinning. Let us then with confidence draw near to the throne of grace, that we may receive mercy and find grace to help in time of need" (Heb. 4:15–16).

That is what we do when we go to reconciliation. Through his ordained priests, Jesus absolves us from our sins and raises us from spiritual death to life; and through the penance required of us we turn our backs on the tomb and set off again toward heaven. Don't let embarrassment over what you have done keep you from truly living!

Risen, Heavenly High Priest

Anointing of the Sick

As Jesus traveled, he sent the Apostles ahead of him to heal the sick (Matt. 10:8). "And they ... anointed with oil many that were sick and healed them" (Mark 6:13). Before his ascension, Jesus said that healings would continue through the Church (Mark 16:17–18). Within a few decades of the resurrection, St. James wrote:

> Is any among you sick? Let him call for the elders [presbyter in Greek] of the Church, and let them pray over him, anointing him with oil in the name of the Lord; and the prayer of faith will save the sick man, and the Lord will raise him up; and if he has committed sins, he will be forgiven. Therefore, confess your sins to one another, and pray for one another, that you may be healed. (James 5:14–16)

Physical healing is a real and ongoing aspect of the Church's mission, one to which we often fail to have recourse. At the same time, we recognize that it is not always God's will. Saint Paul, a conduit of healing for countless others, was told when he prayed for himself, "My grace is sufficient for you, for my power is made perfect in weakness" (2 Cor. 12:9). We recall that Jesus did not heal all the sick of Palestine. The healings he did perform point forward to Jesus's victory over sin, sickness, and death in the resurrection he promises to share with us. (CCC 1505)

When we look at the anointing of the sick in the context of eternity we come to realize that *every* anointing culminates in healing, absolute healing—in the future, when our bodies are raised. In the interim, the sacrament imparts the strength, peace, and courage we need to live with our condition. (CCC 1520) Even this strikes me as a participation in the experience of Jesus when, shortly before his Passion, he, too, was anointed. (Matt. 26:12)

9

Passover Lamb

Jesus's passing over to his Father by his death and Resurrection, the new Passover, is anticipated in the [Last] Supper and celebrated in the Eucharist, which fulfills the Jewish Passover and anticipates the final Passover of the Church in the glory of the kingdom.

⌒CCC 1340

Participation in the Holy Sacrifice of the Mass identifies us with [Jesus's] Heart ... and unites us even now to the Church in heaven.
⌒CCC 1419

The Eucharist is the "source and summit of the Christian life"....
⌒CCC 1324

✛

THE EUCHARIST inserts us into both Jesus's historical sacrifice and the eternal liturgy occurring before God's throne. It is the fulfillment of all the sacrifices of the Old Covenant, but most especially of the Jewish Passover. It was, after all, at a Passover meal that Jesus instituted the Eucharist; and the Eucharist acts as the Passover meal of the New Covenant—the celebration of the Church's passage from the slavery of sin to new life in Christ. Celebrated daily (*tamid*), it is the ultimate way we Christians give thanks (*todah*) to the Father.

In the first section of this chapter, instead of focusing exclusively on Jesus's historical prayer, we will transition back and forth between Jesus's prayer and actions at the Last Supper to his prayer and actions in the Mass today. [1] Our Catholic Faith teaches that Jesus

---

1. The gospels speak to us of the institution of the Eucharist, but give us limited data as to how the Passover was celebrated in the first century. Surprisingly, extra-

worships and offers himself to the Father *in* and *through* the Church! (CCC 1553) He does so through every one of us who takes part, and in a unique way through the bishops and priests who preside. I want you to see how, in the Liturgy of the Eucharist, Jesus makes present, along with himself, the very petitions he prayed at the Last Supper. At the end of the chapter, in the section THE CHURCH AT PRAYER, I will explain how our entire day can be united to the Eucharist, as well as how it sheds light on the traditional Catholic practice of "offering up" life's difficulties, also known as "redemptive suffering."

JESUS'S FINAL PASSOVER
AND THE LITURGY OF THE EUCHARIST

Preparation for the Passover
and the Penitential Rite of the Mass

Every gathering needs nuts-and-bolts preparation. Jesus singled out Peter and John to prepare Passover. It meant procuring the upper room and all of the needed supplies, sacrificing the Passover lamb, and starting the roasting. Because Passover was joined to the Feast of Unleavened Bread (Exod. 12:15), Peter and John also had to make sure that all leavened bread (bread made with yeast) had been removed from the house in which they celebrated.

That final action allowed St. Paul to draw an analogy to the preparation Christians need to make before celebrating the Eucharist. When he discovered that the Corinthian church was tolerant of one of their members living in an illicit sexual relationship, Paul wrote to them, "For Christ, our Paschal Lamb, has been sacrificed. Let us, therefore, celebrate the festival, *not with the old leaven*, the leaven of

biblical sources provide little more; almost everything is gleaned from the Mishna tract *Pesachim*. The reconstruction I provide was synthesized from the following works: Joachim Jeremias, *The Eucharistic Words of Jesus* (Philadelphia: Fortress Press, 1966); Jerome Kodell, *The Eucharist In The New Testament* (Collegeville, MN: The Liturgical Press, 1988); Barry D. Smith, *Jesus's Last Passover Meal* (Lewiston, NY: Mellen Biblical Press, 1993); P. Grelot and J. Pierron, *The Paschal Feast in the Bible* (Baltimore: Helicon, 1966).

malice and evil; but with the unleavened bread of sincerity and truth" (1 Cor. 5:7–8). He drove his point home later in the letter when he wrote, "Whoever, therefore, eats the bread or drinks the cup of the Lord in an unworthy manner will be guilty of profaning the body and blood of the Lord. Let a man examine himself, and so eat of the bread and drink of the cup" (1 Cor. 11:27–28). This is why Mass always begins with a penitential rite. We reflect upon our sins and, as a congregation, confess our wrongdoing and petition the Lord for his mercy.

The upper room Peter and John prepared was much different from what we see portrayed in art. By the first century, Jews had adopted the Greek and Roman banquet style, which meant that the meal was eaten in a reclining position (Luke 22:14) on low couches or cushions. Guests lay on their stomachs and leaned to the left side (think of lying on the floor, your head propped up by your left arm as you watch television), which left their right hand free for eating. Low tables were placed in a U-shape before them, with the inside left open for serving of the next course (as we do for a bridal party at a wedding reception).[2]

The arrangement of Jesus and the Apostles is more than just trivia. It helps to explain why it was perfectly normal for priest and people to face the same direction (East, or *ad orientem*) during the Eucharistic Prayer throughout the Church's first two millennia. Many people, such as myself, grew up hearing the pre-Vatican II liturgy negatively characterized as the priest "turning his back on the people" and "celebrating the Eucharist toward the wall." And yet Jesus and the Apostles would have faced the same direction at the Last Supper.[3]

---

2. By keeping this picture in mind, the Gospel detail about John laying his head back against Jesus's chest (John 13:23–25) is much more intelligible: John would have been to Jesus's right. By leaning back and to the left, his head would have come to rest on Jesus's chest. This reclining position at banquets also helps us understand an event earlier in the gospels, when a woman approached Jesus at a banquet and, "standing *behind him at his feet*, weeping," began to wash his feet with her tears (Luke 7:38).

3. See Joseph Ratzinger, *Spirit of the Liturgy* (San Francisco: Ignatius Press, 2000), 70, 81.

Passover's First Course and the
Eucharist's Presentation of the Gifts and Anamnesis

The first course consisted of lettuce and a simple vinegar dressing for dipping. The words that Jesus chose to inaugurate the supper are incomprehensible apart from some realization of the depths of his love for us. "I have *earnestly desired* to eat this Passover with you before I suffer" (Luke 22:15). He offered a *berakah* over the first of the liturgy's four cups of wine: "Blessed are you, O Lord our God, king of the universe, who created the fruit of the vine."[4] If it sounds familiar, it is because you hear it prayed at Mass, in the Presentation of the Gifts: "Blessed are you, Lord, God of all creation. Through your goodness we have this wine to offer, fruit of the vine and work of human hands. It will become our spiritual drink."[5]

Jesus followed the blessing of the first cup with the Passover Kiddush, or blessing for the feast day. In it, he praised the Father for gathering them in remembrance (*zikkaron* in Hebrew) of their exodus from Egypt. For Jews, *zikkaron* was not a memory exercise. It was a *ceremony* that made a past event present so it could be participated in and the benefits reaped by future generations. While the exodus was a one-time historical event, through the Passover meal every Jew born after that time experienced the exodus; they, too, were set free from bondage in Egypt.

This is expressed in our Eucharistic prayer, too, in a portion following the words of consecration known as the *anamnesis* ("remembrance" in Greek). The priest prays, "Therefore, O Lord, as we now celebrate the memorial of our redemption, we remember Christ's death and his descent to the realm of the dead; we proclaim his Resurrection and his Ascension to your right hand; and as we await his coming in glory, we offer you his Body and Blood, the sacrifice acceptable to you which brings salvation to the whole world."[6]

---

4. Clark, *Introduction to the Eucharist*, 113.
5. *Roman Missal*, 3rd ed., Presentation of the Gifts.
6. Ibid., Eucharistic Prayer IV.

Passover *Haggadah* and the Eucharist's Institution Narrative

As the Passover continued, a second cup of wine and the main course were set before the guests, but they remained untouched. The *haggadah*, or teaching about the significance of the meal and its foods, came first. It was a tradition stretching back to Moses himself. "And when your children say to you, 'What do you mean by this service?' you shall say, 'It is the sacrifice of the LORD's Passover, for he passed over the houses of the sons of Israel in Egypt, when he slew the Egyptians but spared our houses'" (Exod. 12:26–27). Jesus explained why the meal consisted of the foods it did: (1) the Passover Lamb (*Pesach*), whose sacrifice caused God to pass over their houses, (2) unleavened bread (*matzah*), because there was not enough time for the dough they made to rise before the Lord brought redemption, and (3) bitter herbs (*maror*), to remind them of how bitter the Egyptians made their lives.[7]

Jesus and the Apostles then praised God for the way He delivered them by singing the first portion of the *Hallel* (Ps. 113–114): "When Israel went forth from Egypt, the house of Jacob from a people of strange language, Judah became his sanctuary, Israel his dominion. The sea looked and fled, Jordan turned back.... Tremble, O earth, at the presence of the LORD, at the presence of the God of Jacob, who turns the rock into a pool of water, the flint into a spring of water" (Ps. 114:1–3, 7–8).

The only thing left to do before eating commenced was for the host to offer the traditional *berakah* over the bread. "Blessed are you, O Lord our God, King of the universe, who have brought forth bread from the earth."[8] Jesus then surprised everyone by seizing the moment to introduce a new *haggadah*, establishing a new *zikkaron*. "This is my body which is given for you. Do this in remembrance of me" (Luke 22:19). "Given for you"—it was the language of sacrifice.

After the meal, when the third cup of wine was poured, Jesus continued his *haggadah* with the proclamation, "This chalice is the

---

7. Elie Wiesel and Mark Podwal, *A Passover Haggadah* (New York: Simon & Schuster, Inc., 1993), 66–67.

8. We hear this echoed at Mass, during the Presentation of the Gifts.

new covenant in my blood. Do *this*, as often as you drink it, *in remembrance* of me" (1 Cor. 11:25). The Lord told them to celebrate this *ceremony*. Why? Covenants were always initiated with sacrifice. Recall the purpose of sacrifice among the Jews: God and His people were united in the *life* of the sacrificial victim (Lev. 17:11). The sacrifice offered the victim to God, but the people had to take that life into themselves through a covenant meal (Exod. 24:5–11, 12:1–3, 5–10, 13–14). Jesus gave his life to the Father through his Cross, resurrection, and ascension; and he gives it to his people through this new covenant meal.

Jesus had told them this was coming. He chose Passover time (John 6:4) a year or two before to deliver his "Bread of Life" discourse. He told them "my flesh is true food and my blood is true drink. Whoever eats my flesh and drinks my blood remains in me, and I in him. Just as the living Father sent me and I have life because of the Father, so also the one who feeds on me will have life because of me" (John 6:55–57).[9] At the Last Supper, Jesus gave himself—*truly* gave himself—to the Apostles, in what continued to have the appearance of bread and wine. It was the reality for which Israel's entire sacrificial system had served as preparation. Just as the Passover meal allowed every Jew to participate in God's Passover in Egypt, the Eucharist allows us to participate in Jesus's Passover from this world to the Father. The body Jesus gave the Apostles was the same body he offered on the Cross (John 6:51), and the Cross was the *absolute pinnacle of human prayer*!

When our priests today lead us in the eucharistic prayer, the *zikkaron* Jesus commanded, we are taken into these realities. (CCC 1104) Jesus's Last Supper *haggadah* is prayed aloud in our Institution Narrative and the words of consecration.

> **Priest:** For on the night he was betrayed he himself took bread, and giving you thanks he said the blessing, broke the bread and gave it to his disciples, saying:

9. *New American Bible.*

TAKE THIS ALL OF YOU, AND EAT OF IT,
FOR THIS IS MY BODY,
WHICH WILL BE GIVEN UP FOR YOU.

In a similar way, when supper was ended, he took the chalice and giving you thanks he said the blessing, and gave the chalice to his disciples, saying:

TAKE THIS ALL OF YOU, AND DRINK FROM IT,
FOR THIS IS THE CHALICE OF MY BLOOD,
THE BLOOD OF THE NEW AND ETERNAL COVENANT,
WHICH WILL BE POURED OUT FOR YOU AND FOR MANY
FOR THE FORGIVENESS OF SINS.
DO THIS IN MEMORY OF ME.

The mystery of faith.

Priest and People: When we eat this Bread and drink this Cup, we proclaim your Death, O Lord, until you come again.[10]

Our priests, because of the sacrament of holy orders, act *in persona Christi Capitis*, or "in the person of Christ the Head." Jesus uses their lips to pray, "This is my body. [T]his is . . . my blood," transforming the elements on the altar, so that we can receive him in Holy Communion and be united with him to the Father. In the *anamnesis* that follows (recounted earlier), we even hear an echo of Jesus's singing of the *Hallel*—his praise of the mighty work of deliverance the Father accomplished through the Passover.

Jesus's "High Priestly" Prayer and the Intercessions of the Eucharist

John's Gospel records Jesus offering a lengthy prayer at the Last Supper. It is common to hear it called Jesus's "high priestly prayer." He prayed for his Church, first for its leaders, the Apostles,[11] and then for all its future members.

---

10. *Roman Missal*, 3rd ed., Eucharistic Prayer III.

11. Luke 22:31–32 shows Peter, the head of the Apostles, having a special place in Jesus's prayer that night.

[Father,] I have manifested your name to the men whom you gave me out of the world.... I am praying for them;... keep them in your name, which you have given me, that they may be one, even as we are one.... I do not pray for these only, but also for those who will believe in me through their word, that they may all be one; even as you, Father, are in me, and I in you, that they also may be in us, so that the world may believe that you have sent me. (John 17:6, 9, 11, 20–21)

These are the intercessions Christ brings before the Father in our Eucharistic prayer:

May this Sacrifice of our reconciliation, we pray, O Lord, advance the peace and salvation of all the world. Be pleased to confirm in faith and charity your pilgrim Church on earth, with your servant N. our Pope and N. our Bishop, the Order of Bishops, all the clergy, and the entire people you have gained for your own. Listen graciously to the prayers of this family, whom you have summoned before you: in your compassion, O merciful Father, gather to yourself all your children scattered throughout the world.[12]

The eucharistic intercessions are one of the key ways the Church responds to Jesus's invitation to petition the Father in his name: "if you ask anything of the Father, he will give it to you in my name. Until now you have asked nothing in my name; ask, and you will receive" (John 16:23–24).

Conclusion of the Passover and Eucharistic Doxology

Jesus concluded his celebration of the Passover by singing the final portion of the *Hallel* (Ps. 115–118). When you read them, one is immediately struck by the prevalence of the *todah* theme—a thanksgiving sacrifice following deliverance from affliction. Over the centuries, the Holy Spirit had shaped the Passover liturgy so that these words would be on Jesus's lips as he braced himself for Gethsemane and the Cross:

What shall I render to the LORD for all his bounty to me? I will lift up the chalice of salvation and call on the name of the LORD, I

---

12. *Roman Missal*, 3rd ed., Eucharistic Prayer III.

will pay my vows to the LORD in the presence of all his people. Precious in the sight of the LORD is the death of his saints. O LORD, I am your servant; I am your servant, the son of your handmaid. You have loosed my bonds. I will offer to thee the sacrifice of thanksgiving and call on the name of the LORD. (Ps. 116:12–17)

Jesus does this through his priests. Our Eucharistic prayer culminates with the priest lifting up the cup of salvation and the heavenly bread as he gives thanks: "Through him, and with him, and in him, O God, almighty Father, in the unity of the Holy Spirit, all glory and honor is yours, forever and ever."[13]

THE CHURCH AT PRAYER

The Eucharist is the "summit" of our Faith, but it is not a summit to be scaled and then discarded. The union we experience with Jesus, and through him with the entire Trinity, is meant to draw our entire life up toward heaven. Jesus poured himself out to the Father in the Holy Spirit not just at the Cross, but in every moment of his life— every circumstance in which he found himself, in his every thought, word, and action. It is what we Christians are called to also! Saint Paul practically begged his readers in Rome, "present your bodies as a living sacrifice, holy and acceptable to God, which is your spiritual worship" (Rom. 12:1). Like Jesus on the Cross, our actions become *prayer*. Two concrete ways that Catholics do this is (1) the practice of making a "morning offering," and (2) the redemptive value of our sufferings.

The Morning Offering

Beginning in the nineteenth century, the Apostleship of Prayer has encouraged people to start their morning by offering to Jesus everything they will do, or have done to them, that day. Like Jesus on the Cross, our actions and prayer are fused. (CCC 2605) As you read the prayer below, note how it joins the offerer's entire life to the eucha-

13. Ibid., Doxology.

ristic sacrifice, and how it enunciates the intentions carried over from Jesus's high priestly prayer into the intercessions of the eucharistic prayer. It is a wonderful exercise of the common priesthood exercised by all the baptized:

> O Jesus, through the Immaculate Heart of Mary, I offer You my prayers, works, joys, and sufferings of this day in union with the Holy Sacrifice of the Mass throughout the world. I offer them for all the intentions of Your Sacred Heart: the salvation of souls, reparation for sin, and the reunion of all Christians. I offer them for the intentions of our bishops and of all Apostles of Prayer, and in particular for those recommended by our Holy Father this month.

Redemptive Suffering

Saint Paul told the Colossians, "Now I rejoice in my sufferings for your sake, and in my flesh I complete what is lacking in Christ's afflictions for the sake of his body, that is, the Church" (Col. 1:24). It is a mysterious reality to be sure: the suffering God allows into our lives, when accepted and lived with trust in his love, becomes an *actual participation* in the sufferings of the Crucified, allowing us to be formed more truly in his image—the very goal of our Faith. And, as Paul said above, because we are "members of one another" (Rom. 12:5; Eph. 4:25), this grace is of benefit not just to us, but to the entire body. This teaching, far from casting aspersions on the efficacy of Jesus's sacrifice, proclaims its superabundance. We believe that Jesus's sacrifice redeems us so profoundly that it transforms us from mere creatures of God into sons and daughters. It transforms us into cells of Jesus's mystical body, *inserting us* into the life, death, resurrection, and ascension of the *only Son*. This reality is there in the theology of Paul, and unpacked for us in the teaching of the saints and doctors. What we might not see is how it is contained in Jesus's institution of the Eucharist. Let me explain.

"This is my body. . . . This is my blood." From whom did Jesus receive his body and blood? From his mother Mary. He clothed himself with her flesh, her blood, and offered himself to the Father "in" them. That is the mystery of redemptive suffering that the Lord wants to continue in you and me—to clothe himself with our very persons and lift our sufferings up into his own, making them part of his eternal offering to the Father (Heb. 9:14). As with Mary, he requires our consent to bring about this supernatural reality. "I am the handmaid of the Lord; let it be to me according to your word" (Luke 1:38).

We see Mary, fully engaged in this mystery, at the foot of her Son's Cross. Which of us parents haven't imagined looking up and seeing our own children hanging there in the sun—their bodies torn, blood flowing down their limbs, suffocating under their own weight. It is the most monstrous suffering imaginable, but God allowed it into the life of his beloved Mary. Her Son was dying to redeem the world, and her heart was pierced right along with his (John 19:34; Luke 2:35). Jesus was suffering there before her eyes, in the flesh he took from her; but through the cords of grace he was suffering in and through her person gazing up at him as well. Through it all, the Holy Spirit maintained Mary in her *fiat*: "let it be to me according to your word"; and Scripture tells us that she shared her Son's suffering. "[Mary,] a sword will pierce through your own soul also" (Luke 2:35). The mystery of redemptive suffering spoken of by Paul in Colossians 1:24 is graphically manifested by Mary at the Cross.

We Catholics don't see any romance in pain, and we don't desire it; but part of reality is recognizing that God allows us to pass through it. It is not an end in itself, but a potentially powerful means: "For [Jesus's] sake I have suffered the loss of all things, and count them as refuse, in order that I may gain Christ and be found in him . . . that I may know him and the power of his resurrection, and may share his sufferings, becoming like him in his death, that if possible I may attain the resurrection from the dead" (Phil. 3:8–11). So we need to call out for the grace to unite our sufferings to those of Jesus, to allow him to lift us up toward his Father. "This is my body. . . . This is my blood." We need to pray each day for the grace to persevere through suffering; Jesus told us the stakes are high: "because wickedness is multiplied, most men's love will grow cold. But he who endures to the end will be saved" (Matt. 24:12–13).

10

The Heart of Prayer

[Jesus] has loved us all with a human heart. For this reason, the Sacred Heart of Jesus, pierced for our sins and for our salvation, is "quite rightly considered the chief sign and symbol of that . . . love with which the divine Redeemer continually loves the eternal Father and all human beings" without exception. ⟶CCC 478

The whole prayer of Jesus is contained in this loving adherence of his human heart to the mystery of the will of the Father. ⟶CCC 2603

✛

JESUS'S SACRED HEART is one of the most easily identified symbols of Catholicism. Practice of the traditional devotions in honor of the Sacred Heart has, however, undergone a drastic decline in the last fifty years. That should be cause for alarm because, as we have seen throughout the course of this book, Jesus's heart was the "organ" of his prayer, and the practices associated with this devotion provide practical and powerful means for uniting our entire lives to his prayer!

The Sacred Heart devotion is one of the beautiful fruits drawn from the Church's 2,000 years of meditation and contemplation. The revelation, the deposit of Faith Jesus entrusted to the Church was so profound that we are still unfolding its implications today. What does it mean to practice devotion to Jesus's heart? Let us look at how devotion to Jesus's heart evolved over the centuries, and the ideas and themes it expressed for its practitioners.

DEVOTION TO JESUS'S HEART

A Deepening Realization

The Church's early centuries were times of conflict. The Church battled a number of heresies regarding Jesus's divinity and humanity. The Holy Spirit, however, brought good out of it. Heresies forced the Church's shepherds to fall back upon the Holy Spirit, to gaze long and hard into the revelation with which they had been entrusted, and to articulate the Faith more clearly as a result. This was how the Nicene-Constantinopolitan Creed, the Church's *Shema*, came about.

The Councils of Nicaea, Constantinople, Ephesus, and Chalcedon drew together and enunciated the great truths about Jesus present, but diffuse, in Scripture and Tradition: He was not one of the Father's spiritual creations, but of the same "substance," one in being, with the Father. Without surrendering his divinity, God the Son *became* a *true human being*. He has a human body *and a human soul* (mind, will, and their mysterious center, the heart).

During its first millennia, the Church contemplated a number of elements that would eventually be drawn together by the devotion.[1] The first was its meditation on Jesus as the source of the living water, the Spirit (John 7:37–39). The Church recognized that the Spirit was released by the piercing of Jesus's side, as the blood and water issued forth (John 19:34; 1 John 5:6–8). This element appeared early, in the writings of Justin Martyr (AD 155), Irenaeus (ca. 185), Hippolytus of Rome (204), and Cyprian (250).

Saint Paul identified Jesus as the new Adam (Rom. 5:12–19; 1 Cor. 15:21–22). Adam's bride was formed when the Lord put Adam into a deep sleep and removed a rib from his side, forming Eve. Tertullian, writing ca. AD 210, understood that "[i]f Adam is a type of Christ then Adam's sleep is a symbol of the death of Christ and by the wound in the side of Christ was formed the Church, the true Mother of all the living."[2] Saints Augustine and John Chrysostom

---

1. For this section, I am completely indebted to Timothy O'Donnell, *The Heart of the Redeemer* (San Francisco: Ignatius Press), 79–92.

2. Tertullian's *The Soul*, quoted in O'Donnell, *The Heart of the Redeemer*, 84.

perceived the water and blood issuing from Jesus's side to be the sacraments of initiation: baptism and the Eucharist.

The early Church was firm in its conviction that Jesus suffered willingly, out of love for us. "The Son of God . . . loved me and gave himself for me" (Gal. 2:20). It also understood that this suffering was not just in Jesus's body, but also in his spirit. "My soul is very sorrowful, even to death" (Mark 14:34–35). And in his suffering, Jesus sought consolation in friends who would watch and pray. "Simon, are you asleep? Could you not watch one hour? Watch and pray. . . ." (Mark 14:37–38). We find St. Hilary of Poitiers (ca. AD 365) and Hesychius of Jerusalem (ca. 450) meditating on these themes.[3]

The final element streaming toward the Sacred Heart devotion was the Church's veneration of the Apostle John. His Gospel, much more so than the others, soared upward in considering Jesus's divinity. John was also gifted with the profound insight that "God is love" (1 John 4:8). What allowed him to penetrate Jesus's mystery so deeply? Meditation led the Church (especially Pope St. Gregory) to recognize that it was John's intense love of the Lord, revealed in the gesture of resting his head upon Jesus's breast at the Last Supper (John 13:23).

These insights percolated in the minds of saints and whole religious orders as the Church grew into the Middle Ages. By the early 1100s, St. Bernard of Clairvaux made frequent mention not only of our Lord's pierced side, but also of the pierced heart within, symbol of Jesus's suffering love. The first apparition in which Jesus showed his heart to someone was also recorded: St. Lutgard of St. Trond reported that Jesus "exchanged" hearts with her.[4] By the twelfth century, the Dominicans and Franciscans, with their passionate love of our Lord's humanity, were spreading devotion to the Sacred Heart among the laity. Saint Bonaventure, a Franciscan friar, drew a powerful application from St. Paul's teaching about the mystical body: "I say without hesitation that His heart is also mine. Since Christ is my head, how could that which belongs to my head not also belong to me?"[5] Saint

---

3. Ibid., 90.
4. Ibid., 97.
5. Ibid., 101.

Albert the Great, a Dominican, did the same with the early Church's insight as to how the sacraments sprang from Jesus's *pierced side*; Albert made explicit that they sprang from his *pierced heart*.

Three Benedictine nuns—St. Mechtild of Madeburg, St. Mechtild of Hackeborn, and St. Gertrude the Great—were tremendously influential in spreading devotion to Jesus's heart. Residents of the same German convent, each had a number of mystical experiences. Two of St. Gertrude's apparitions speak to our desire of participating in Jesus's prayer: Once, when Gertrude was angry with herself over her imperfections in praying the Liturgy of the Hours, our Lord showed her his heart and said,

> I manifest to the gaze of thy soul My deified Heart, the harmonious instrument whose sweet tones ravish the Most Adorable Trinity. I give It to thee, and like a faithful, zealous servant, this Heart will be ready, at any moment, to repair thy defects and negligences. . . . Make use of It and thy works will charm the eye and ear of the Divinity.[6]

At another time she reported seeing his heart "as an altar upon which the sacrifices of the faithful, the homage of the elect, and the worship of the Angels are offered, and on which Jesus, the Eternal High Priest, offers Himself in sacrifice."[7]

The Lord granted the next phase of development to his French saints. Saint Francis de Sales, famous for his *Introduction to the Devout Life*, spoke and wrote on the Sacred Heart frequently. Saint Jean Eudes, founder of the Congregation of Our Lady of Charity and the Society of Jesus and Mary, was inspired to bring the Sacred Heart into the Church's liturgical life. He wrote Masses in honor of the hearts of both Jesus and Mary and received permission for his congregations to celebrate them. In time bishops granted permission for their celebration in their diocese. Listen to one of St. Jean's meditations on the Sacred Heart:

---

6. *Gertrude the Great: Herald of Divine Love* (Rockford, IL: TAN Books and Publishers, Inc., 1989), 28–29.
   7. Ibid., 27.

It is the uncreated and eternal love, namely, the Holy Spirit who has built this magnificent Temple and built it from the virginal blood of the Mother of love. . . . It is infinitely holier than any temple, material or spiritual, ever built. . . . It is in that Temple that God receives adorations, praises and glory worthy of his infinite greatness.

But the love of Jesus is not only a temple: it is also the altar of divine love. It is on that altar that the sacred fire of that same love is burning night and day. It is on that altar that our High Priest Jesus continually offers sacrifices to the most Holy Trinity.[8]

Jean-Jacques Olier, founder of the Sulpicians, brought together a number of scriptural themes in his reflection on the Sacred Heart and prayer:

What can be said of the glory that God's majesty receives from the Heart of Jesus alone, that Heart which gives more homage to God than do all the saints? For saints and angels are made to express the feelings and thoughts of the Heart of Jesus.

All the praise and respect that the saints have ever rendered to God are drawn from the Heart of Jesus Christ, and from His fullness. . . . It is this great Heart that holds all that is poured out so lavishly in the Church. [It] is the source of our religion, source too and plenitude of our homage to God.[9]

Jean-Jacques anticipated the theme of this book by almost 400 years!

St. Margaret Mary Alacoque

The development of devotion to the Sacred Heart reached a kind of "critical mass" on Dec. 27, 1673, the Feast of St. John the Evangelist. It was on that date that the Lord began a series of revelations to a young nun in the Convent of the Visitation at Paray-le-Monial, France—St. Margaret Mary Alacoque. The revelations persisted over a number of years, but four principle ones are spoken of with

---

8. St. John Eudes's *Meditations on Various Subjects*, quoted in O'Donnell, *The Heart of the Redeemer*, 121.

9. O'Donnell, *The Heart of the Redeemer*, 121–22.

regard to the Sacred Heart devotion. The first, coming on the Feast of St. John, consisted in the Lord placing her head on his breast, as St. John's had been, and communicating to her both the unfathomable love of his heart as well as the mission of making it known to a world engulfed in sin. He called her "the disciple of my Sacred Heart."

During the second apparition, Margaret Mary wrote that she saw Jesus's heart

> as on a throne of flames, more brilliant than the sun and as transparent as crystal. It had Its adorable wound and was encircled with a crown of thorns, which signifies the pain our sins caused Him. It was surmounted by a cross which signified that . . . from the time this Sacred Heart was formed, the cross was planted in It. . . .[10]

The Lord impressed upon her that, "under the symbol of this Heart of flesh," an image he wanted publicly venerated, he intended to draw men and women of "these last centuries" to himself. "This devotion was as a last effort of His love."[11]

The third and principal apparition was in 1674, during the Octave of the Feast of Corpus Christi (the Body and Blood of Christ). She wrote how Jesus

> presented Himself to me all resplendent with glory, His five wounds shining like so many suns. Flames issued from every part of His sacred humanity, especially from His adorable Breast, which resembled a furnace, which being opened disclosed to me His most loving and loveable Heart, which was the living source of the flames.

> [He] showed to me to what an excess He had loved men, from whom He received only ingratitude and contempt. "I feel this more," He said, "than all I suffered in my Passion. If only they would make me some return for my love. . . . Do you at least console me by supplying for their ingratitude, as far as you can."[12]

10. Francis Larkin, *Enthronement of the Sacred Heart* (Boston: Daughters of St. Paul, 1978), 28.
11. Ibid., 28–29.
12. Ibid., 29–30.

When Margaret Mary began to assert her unworthiness and inability, Jesus replied, "Behold, this will supply for all that is wanting in you." Then from his open heart "there issued a flame so ardent that I thought I should be consumed, for I was wholly penetrated with it."[13] That is the theology of grace writ large!

The fourth apparition occurred in June, 1675. As Margaret Mary prayed before the Blessed Sacrament, our Lord showed her his heart, saying:

> Behold this Heart which has loved men so much, that It has spared nothing even to exhausting and consuming Itself in order to testify to them Its love; and in return I receive from the greater number nothing but ingratitude by reason of their irreverence and sacrileges, and by the coldness and contempt they show me *in this Sacrament of Love....*[14]

The Lord then asked that a new feast, one honoring his Sacred Heart, be established on the Friday following the Feast of Corpus Christi. He requested that the faithful attend Mass and receive Communion on that day in reparation for the indignities and sacrilege he suffered while exposed upon the altars—especially those inflicted upon him by baptized Christians, and by priests in particular.

As I said, St. Margaret Mary received revelations over a number of years. Scattered throughout her writings, one finds promises the Lord made to those who take up the devotion. Not meant to be exhaustive, one often hears of the Twelve Promises of the Sacred Heart. These can be found in Appendix III, along with scriptural references.

To assist Margaret Mary in her mission, the Lord sent her two gifted collaborators—the Jesuits St. Claude de la Colombiere and Fr. Jean Croiset. Both served as her spiritual directors. Saint Claude preached the Sacred Heart devotion in France and England, and Fr. Croiset wrote *The Devotion to the Sacred Heart of Jesus*. Saint Margaret Mary gave the book her strongest approval, writing, "[In] your

13. Ibid., 30
14. Ibid., 31

117

work on the adorable Heart of my Jesus, I have no doubt that He has assisted you, since the whole work, if I be not mistaken, is so perfectly in accordance with His wishes, that I do not think that it will be necessary to change anything in it. . . ."[15]

Fr. Croiset summarized the devotion in this way: "The particular object of this devotion is the immense love of the Son of God, which induced Him to deliver Himself up to death for us and to give Himself entirely to us in the Blessed Sacrament of the altar."[16] "Love is its object, love its motive and principle, and it is love that ought to be its end."[17] Father Croiset asks, "Do we remember that the Sacred Heart of Jesus in the Blessed Sacrament has . . . the same sentiments as it always has had: that It is always burning with love for us, always sensibly touched by the evils that befall us, always urged by the desire to make us share in His treasures. . . ?"[18]

This brings us to the call the Lord made for reparation. During his earthly life, the Spirit poured from Jesus's divine nature, inflamed his human heart, and found expression in the baptism of repentance he received from John as well as the prayer and fasting he engaged in on behalf of his rebellious people. The Sacred Heart devotion reminds us, in an urgent way, that we are called to share in the reparation made by our Head. Jesus showed Margaret Mary that we do not make reparation on our own, but as members of his body, animated by the Spirit that inflames his own human heart. We live in an age when only a fraction of baptized Catholics attend Sunday Mass. And of those who do, how many receive Communion while in open dissent from Church teaching? How many receive in a state of mortal sin? How many of us, so proud to profess belief in Jesus's Real Presence, make time outside of Mass to visit him in the Tabernacle? *Serious reparation is needed.* "You are the body of Christ. [I]f one member suffers, all suffer together" (1 Cor. 12:27, 26). The Sacred Heart devotion is a prayer of reparation—the Lord

---

15. Jean Croiset, *The Devotion to the Sacred Heart of Jesus* (Rockford, IL: TAN Books and Publishers, Inc., 1988), xii.

16. Ibid., 53.

17. Ibid., 55.

18. Ibid., 77.

calls us to unite ourselves with him in the Eucharist. We are to offer ourselves through, with, and in him on behalf of our many brothers and sisters who do not.

In the years following the revelations made to St. Margaret Mary and the missions of St. Claude and Fr. Croiset, the Feast of the Sacred Heart was established in the universal Church. And the image of Jesus's heart—pierced by the lance, encircled with thorns, the Cross driven into it, and yet *alive*, aflame with love both human and divine—is known throughout the world. Devotion to the Sacred Heart has even been taken up and extolled to the whole Church by the successors of Peter in the encyclicals *On Consecration to the Sacred Heart* (*Annum Sacrum*, 1899), *On Reparation to the Sacred Heart* (*Miserentissimus Redemptor*, 1928), and *On Devotion to the Sacred Heart* (*Haurietis Aquas*, 1956).

Concretely, How Does This Enrich Our Prayer?

More intense participation in the Eucharist and renewed wonder at both the Incarnation and the physical and spiritual sufferings Jesus endured for love of us are channels of transformative grace. The goal is for our entire life, every aspect of it, to enter into his Eucharist, his Passover to the Father. Saint Margaret Mary wrote of how Jesus commanded her to "make a donation to Him of all that was in me capable of pleasing Him, of all that I could do or suffer to the end of my life and of all the good works that others might do for me."[19] In the language of the spiritual life, such an act is called *consecration*. (The last chapter's Morning Offering is an example.)

Consecration means to take something out of the "world" and set it completely apart for God's use. With Jesus we offer back to the Father all that we have received from him. It was part of Jesus's high priestly prayer for us: "[Father,] for their sake I consecrate myself, that *they also may be consecrated* in truth" (John 17:19). Saint Paul spoke of it: "present your bodies as a living sacrifice, holy and acceptable to God, which is your spiritual worship" (Rom. 12:1). It

19. Ibid., 37.

is living Christianity to the full, truly becoming "partakers of the divine nature" (2 Pet. 1:4).

It is axiomatic to say that Jesus was always in prayer, always communing with the Father. Just like us, though, he was also engaged in the tasks of everyday life. Three times a day, he prayed the Eighteen Benedictions. He spent whole nights in prayer upon the mountains. But how did he pray when he was carrying on a conversation with a customer in the carpentry shop? "According to Scripture, it is the *heart* that prays."[20] In the highest part of his soul, his gaze never left the Father. His "conscious" mind may have been thinking upon work or play, but his core, his heart, never left the Father. I would suggest that, by God's grace, this can be true of us as well.

In our first chapter we read St. Paul's mysterious words on prayer: "the Spirit himself intercedes for us with sighs too deep for words. And [the Father] who searches the hearts of men knows what is the mind of the Spirit, because the Spirit intercedes for the saints according to the will of God" (Rom. 8:26–27). Jesus's human heart, *aflame with the Spirit*, perpetually offered itself to the Father no matter what other activity he was engaged in. This prayer of the Spirit that Paul says is going on within us is nothing less than *the prayer of the Sacred Heart on our behalf and that of the world.*

At the dawn of his human life, our Lord prayed, "Behold, I come. . . . I delight to do your will, O my God; your law is within my heart" (Ps. 40:7–8). If we want to consciously unite ourselves with his offering, then we should begin each day with an act of consecration, a renewal of the gift of self made to God in baptism. There are many beautiful prayers of consecration that can be used, or we can offer ourselves to the Lord very simply, in our own words. Our intent should be to offer Jesus our hearts, souls, bodies, joys, and sufferings and to hold nothing back for ourselves. Saint Therese of Lisieux discovered an ingenious way to constantly renew her prayer of consecration, even in her sleep: "O my Beloved, I desire at every beat of my heart to renew this Oblation an infinite number of times."

When we do this, all our thoughts, words, and actions are converted into prayer. We live our day intent on performing God's will

20. CCC 2562.

for us—taking care of children, going to work, cleaning the house, assisting those in need. We still make time—ideally every morning, afternoon, and evening—for conscious vocal and mental prayer (Scripture, Rosary, Stations of the Cross, conversation with God, etc.). Throughout the day we thank the Lord for the blessings and helps we're given, offering little petitions as needs arise ("Lord, please help me find that file"). All of these are transformed into acts of reparative love on behalf of the body. This is how we fulfill Scripture's directive to "pray constantly." (1 Thess. 5:17; see CCC 2745) If you put this into practice, don't be surprised to find your mind turning to the Lord ever more frequently, to find yourself addressing him interiorly while doing dishes or cleaning the bathroom.

When so much of life is a vicious circle, consecration to Jesus's heart leads us in a glorious upward spiral—from more intense participation in the Eucharist, to a day animated by prayer, back to the Eucharist, and so on, and so on, until we take our place in the liturgy of Heaven.

THE CHURCH AT PRAYER

Litany of the Sacred Heart

Like the larger devotion, this litany took shape over centuries. Its final form is evidence of great thought: thirty-three invocations of our Lord's human heart, one for each year it prayed here on earth:

V. Lord, have mercy on us.

R. Christ, have mercy on us.

V. Lord, have mercy on us. Christ, hear us.

R. Christ, graciously hear us.

V. God the Father of Heaven, *have mercy on us.*

God the Son, Redeemer of the world, *have mercy on us.*

God the Holy Spirit, *have mercy on us.*

Holy Trinity, one God, *have mercy on us.*

Heart of Jesus, Son of the Eternal Father, *have mercy on us.*

Heart of Jesus, formed by the Holy Spirit in the Virgin Mother's womb...

Heart of Jesus, substantially united to the Word of God...

Heart of Jesus, of infinite majesty...

Heart of Jesus, holy Temple of God...

Heart of Jesus, Tabernacle of the Most High...

Heart of Jesus, house of God and gate of heaven...

Heart of Jesus, glowing furnace of charity...

Heart of Jesus, vessel of justice and love...

Heart of Jesus, full of goodness and love...

Heart of Jesus, abyss of all virtues...

Heart of Jesus, most worthy of all praise...

Heart of Jesus, King and center of all hearts...

Heart of Jesus, in whom are all the treasures of wisdom and knowledge...

Heart of Jesus, in whom dwells all the fullness of the Godhead...

Heart of Jesus, in whom the Father was well pleased...

Heart of Jesus, of whose fullness we have all received...

Heart of Jesus, desire of the everlasting hills...

Heart of Jesus, patient and rich in mercy...

Heart of Jesus, rich to all who call upon You...

Heart of Jesus, fount of life and holiness...

Heart of Jesus, propitiation for our offenses...

Heart of Jesus, overwhelmed with reproaches...

Heart of Jesus, bruised for our iniquities...

Heart of Jesus, obedient even unto death...

Heart of Jesus, pierced with a lance...

Heart of Jesus, source of all consolation...

Heart of Jesus, our life and resurrection...

Heart of Jesus, our peace and reconciliation...

Heart of Jesus, victim for our sins...

Heart of Jesus, salvation of those who hope in You…

Heart of Jesus, hope of those who die in You…

Heart of Jesus, delight of all saints…

V. Lamb of God, who takest away the sins of the world,

R. Spare us, O Lord.

V. Lamb of God, who takest away the sins of the world,

R. Graciously hear us, O Lord.

V. Lamb of God, who takest away the sins of the world,

R. Have mercy on us.

V. Jesus, meek and humble of Heart,

R. Make our hearts like unto Thine.

Let us pray.

Almighty and eternal God, look upon the Heart of Thy most beloved Son and upon the praises and satisfaction which He offers Thee in the name of sinners; and to those who implore Thy mercy, in Thy great goodness, grant forgiveness in the name of the same Jesus Christ, Thy Son, who livest and reignest with Thee forever and ever. Amen.

11

Mary in the Prayer Life
of Jesus and the Church

In prayer the Holy Spirit unites us to the person of the only Son, in his glorified humanity, through which and in which our filial prayer unites us in the Church with the Mother of Jesus. ⁓CCC 2673

Mary is the perfect Orans *(pray-er), a figure of the Church. [L]ike the beloved disciple we welcome Jesus's mother into our homes. . . .* ⁓CCC 2679

ANYONE WHO HAS started making a daily act of consecration knows that it is one thing to pray the prayer, and quite another to live it out. The prayers, thoughts, words, and actions we offer to the Father through Jesus are marred not just by immaturity and imperfections, but sin. Jesus's pristine love repairs for our shortcomings, but Jesus is absolutely clear that we must grow to spiritual adulthood (Matt. 5:48; John 15:1–2).

To help us on our way, Jesus gave us the same gift the Father gave him—the Blessed Mother. "When Jesus saw his mother, and the disciple whom he loved standing near, he said to his mother, 'Woman, behold, your son!' Then he said to the disciple, 'Behold, your mother!' And from that hour the disciple took her to his own home" (John 19:26–27). John served as the proxy for all of Jesus's beloved disciples; Mary is the mother of the whole mystical body (Rev. 12:1–5, 17). She assists us in three key ways: by her example, through the communication of grace, and in prayer.

Her Example

Thinking about our Blessed Mother, it occurs to me that Jesus's life and prayer were projected backward into hers: his freedom from sin was communicated to her in the Immaculate Conception. His prayer in the Garden of Gethsemane was already on her lips at the annunciation (Luke 1:38). Before Jesus used the example of a tireless widow to teach about prayer (Luke 18:1–5), his widowed mother was at Cana, petitioning him for his first sign—and apparently refusing to take "no" for an answer (John 2:1–11)!

Not only this, but she was his daily prayer partner—sometimes three times a day—for thirty years. For nine months his Sacred Heart beat beneath her own. *Mary taught him human prayer!* (CCC 2599) The flesh he offered in sacrifice came from her! She is the model contemplative with her eyes fixed on Jesus, constantly pondering everything he said and did (Luke 2:19, 51). No one has participated in his prayer the way she did, and she did it while living the busy life of a wife, mother, and homemaker. And at the end of her life she was assumed into heaven body and soul, caught up into her Son's resurrection and ascension. She is the Church's preeminent member, anticipating the glory destined for the entire body at the end of history.

Consecration To Jesus Through Mary

I'm sure you've heard the principle "Work smarter, not harder." It applies to the spiritual life just as much as it does to careers or to body building. It was the principle that inspired St. Louis de Montfort to pen *True Devotion to the Blessed Virgin*. De Montfort's thesis was that, just as Mary was the conduit by which Jesus came to us, she is the most perfect means of going to him.

We're each called to take on the image of Christ. De Montfort reminds us that there are two ways to make an image, a statue. The first is to get a block of marble and go at it with hammer and chisel—an apt image for the way many of us feel about God's "pruning" (John 15:2; Heb. 12:5–13). The second way is much easier: pour material into a mold and allow it to harden. De Montfort saw Mary's womb as the mold, and our souls the material that needs shaping into the image of Jesus.

When I first heard his thesis twenty years ago, I was uncomfortable, to say the least. It sounded like all of Protestantism's worst fears about Catholics and Mary had come true. *Mary helping to shape us?* What eventually caused me to crack the book open was discovering how many of the twentieth century's spiritual giants, like St. Maximilian Kolbe and Bd. John Paul II, made it the hallmark of their spirituality. Blessed John Paul's papal motto "Totus Tuus," or "all yours [Mary]," was even a quotation from it! Challenged by this, I humbled myself and asked the Holy Spirit to open my eyes to what, if anything, he wanted me to see in the book. That was a dangerous prayer, because I now find myself rereading at least a portion every year.

Saint Louis began by establishing Mary's position in relation to God. "With the whole Church I acknowledge that Mary, being a mere creature fashioned by the hand of God is, compared to his infinite majesty, less than an atom, or rather is simply nothing, since he alone can say, 'I am he who is.'"[1] Nevertheless, before an atom of the universe came into existence, she was predestined to be the Mother of God, the most exalted person in creation, next to her Son. And yet she practiced perfect humility. She understood that all the gifts and virtues she possessed came from God's hand, and that she could call nothing her own. Her whole life was at the service of her divine Son.

I really appreciated the way de Montfort answered detractors of his Marian devotion during his lifetime. He took their complaints to Jesus in a series of rhetorical questions: "Does Mary keep for herself any honor we pay her? Is she a rival of yours? Is she a stranger having no kinship with you? Does pleasing her imply displeasing you? Does the gift of oneself to her constitute a deprivation for you? Is love for her a lessening of our love for you?"[2] Put in those terms, the answer is obvious.

At the heart of de Montfort's Marian devotion is an idea we are already familiar with: consecration—but with a twist. "All perfec-

---

1. Louis Marie de Montfort, *True Devotion to the Blessed Virgin* (Bay Shore, NY: Montfort Publications, 1996), no. 14.
2. Ibid., no. 64.

tion consists in our being conformed, united, and consecrated to Jesus. . . . Now of all God's creatures Mary is the most conformed to Jesus. It therefore follows that, of all devotions, devotion to her makes for the most effective consecration and conformity to him. The more one is consecrated to Mary, the more one is consecrated to Jesus."[3] De Montfort grounds our ability to make such a consecration in the doctrine of the communion of saints, Christ's mystical body.

It is a development, to be sure, but I am convinced that it is firmly rooted in Scripture. The Apostle Peter wrote, "like living stones be yourselves built into a spiritual house . . . to offer spiritual sacrifices acceptable to God through Jesus Christ" (1 Pet. 2:4–5). The Apostle Paul developed it further, teaching that "we, though many, are one body in Christ, and individually *members of one another*" (Rom. 12:5). Fused to Jesus, we find ourselves, at the level of the soul, mysteriously joined to one another. We already saw, when we looked at reparation and redemptive suffering, how far this reality extends. The grace that God gives to one member of the body can be of benefit to all.

If this is true of you and me, then how much more so of Mary? The angel Gabriel called her the *Kecharitomene*, the one who is "completely filled" with God's grace. The grace God gave allowed her to overcome every difficulty and offer herself to Him without reserve. She said "yes" so completely that Jesus became physically incarnate in her. Mary is the living stone I want to be fitted to, the cell of Christ's body alongside of which I want to be functioning. I want the grace in Mary's soul, so that I can give a "yes" like hers. Look at the effect Mary's arrival had on the home of Elizabeth and John the Baptist: "when Elizabeth heard the greeting of Mary, the child leaped in her womb; and Elizabeth was filled with the Holy Spirit" (Luke 1:41). That's why Jesus told John and all us other beloved disciples to take Mary into *our homes*.

Go back to the Old Testament, to Elijah and Elisha. Before he was taken up in the fiery chariot, Elijah told his pupil to ask a favor of

---

3. Ibid., no. 120.

him. Elisha's request? "I pray you, let me inherit a double share of your spirit" (2 Kings 2:9); and that was exactly what Elisha got! Now as mother of the Incarnate Word, it would be impossible for us to receive a "double" portion of Mary's spirit, as she possesses more grace than all saints and angels combined. But the Holy Spirit and Mary do want us to participate in it! They want us to tap into it to accelerate our spiritual growth. Again, as Paul said, "we are members of one another." She isn't the mother of just Jesus the individual, but of his whole mystical body (John 19:26–27; Rev. 12:17). She gave birth to and nourished Jesus, and the most efficient means for growth in Christ is to allow her to do it for us, too.

When we consecrate ourselves to Jesus, through Mary, we are, in effect, asking the Holy Spirit to "knit" our souls to Mary's. We want to participate in *her consecration to Jesus*. We want to share the virtues adorning her soul: her faith, humility, obedience, perseverance, and love. We even want to share in her most beautiful grace, that of being completely fluid in the hands of the Spirit, so that he can form Christ Jesus in the womb of our souls. Saint Louis spoke of doing all things through, with, and in Mary "in order to do them more perfectly *through* Jesus, *with* Jesus, [and] *in* Jesus" (emphasis in the original).[4]

De Montfort composed a lengthy prayer of consecration—a renewal of our baptismal promises, with Mary standing at our side, before her Son. It is preceded by thirty-three days of spiritual exercises, and renewed frequently thereafter by a simple prayer, such as "I am all yours, Jesus, through your mother Mary."

The Perfect Prayer Partner

At the time of his ascension, Jesus instructed the Apostles to return to Jerusalem and await the gift of the Spirit. In the nine days that followed, they "devoted themselves to prayer, together with the women and *Mary the mother of Jesus*" (Acts 1:14). It was the Church's first novena, with the result being *Pentecost*! We want Mary praying with us, too.

4. Ibid., no. 257.

THE CHURCH AT PRAYER

The Church has given us many prayers asking Mary's intercession. The most ancient, of course, is the *Hail Mary*. It is a petition ("Holy Mary, Mother of God, pray for us sinners now and at the hour of our death") preceded by the words spoken to Mary by Gabriel ("Hail, full of grace, the Lord is with thee," Luke 1:28) and Elizabeth ("Blessed are you among women, and blessed is the fruit of your womb," Luke 1:42). The *Hail Mary* plays a large part in the Rosary, which we will explore in a moment. First, let us look at the *Angelus* and *Regina Coeli*.

The Angelus

This devotion, which consists of marking the day with three times of prayer, is reminiscent of the Jewish prayer regimen practiced by Jesus and Mary (especially in their shared times in Nazareth). The Angelus is accompanied by the ringing of a church bell (6 AM, noon, and 6 PM), just as the *shofar* was blown to announce the opening and closing of the Temple gate! When we pray the *Angelus* (Latin for "angel"), we celebrate our Lord's Incarnation by recalling three verses of Scripture, following each with the *Hail Mary*: (1) "The angel of the Lord declared unto Mary. And she conceived by the Holy Spirit" (paraphrase of Luke 1:35); (2) "Behold the handmaid of the Lord. Be it done unto me according to thy Word" (Luke 1:38); (3) "And the Word was made flesh. And dwelt among us." (John 1:14) There is no mincing of words in the *Angelus*. It is a brief means, in union with Mary, of renewing our consecration to Jesus throughout the day.

Regina Coeli

During the Easter Season (Holy Saturday through Pentecost Sunday), the Church prays the *Regina Coeli* (Latin for "Queen of Heaven") in place of the *Angelus*. Composed more than 900 years ago, it unites our hearts to Mary's in the communion of saints and shares *her joy* over Jesus's resurrection:

> Queen of Heaven, rejoice, alleluia.
> For He whom you did merit to bear, alleluia.
> Has risen, as He said, alleluia.

Pray for us to God, alleluia.
Rejoice and be glad, O Virgin Mary, alleluia.
For the Lord has truly risen, alleluia.

Let us pray.

O God, who have been pleased to gladden the world
by the resurrection of your Son our Lord Jesus Christ,
grant, we pray, that through his Mother, the Virgin Mary,
we may receive the joys of everlasting life.
Through the same Christ our Lord. Amen.

The Rosary

The Acts of the Apostles tell us that the Apostles prepared for Pentecost by spending time with Mary in prayer. Of what did their prayer
consist? Petition, combined with a great deal of *meditation*—thinking and rethinking the things Jesus had said to them, the actions
and miracles they witnessed, the meaning of his death, resurrection,
and ascension. It consisted of reflecting upon Scripture; when Jesus
appeared to them on the night of his resurrection, he had "opened
their minds to understand the Scriptures, . . . the law of Moses and
the prophets and the psalms" and how they had been fulfilled in
him (Luke 24:44–45). And this meditation was being done *in the
presence of Mary*. She was engaged in it with them. Listen to Bd.
John Paul II's insight here:

> Mary lived with her eyes fixed on Christ, treasuring his every word:
> "She kept all these things, pondering them in her heart" (Luke
> 2:19; cf. 2:51). The memories of Jesus, impressed upon her heart,
> were always with her, leading her to reflect on the various moments
> of her life at her Son's side. In a way those memories were to be the
> "rosary" which she recited uninterruptedly throughout her earthly
> life.[5]

The Apostles spent nine days engaged in this with her, making
the Church's first novena. We can see the fruits that emerged: Peter's

5. Blessed John Paul II, *Rosarium Virginis Mariae*, no. 11. http://www.vatican.va/
holy_father/john_paul_ii/apost_letters/documents/hf_jp-ii_apl_20021016_rosariu
m-virginis-mariae_en.html.

move to replace the office left vacant by Judas's defection emerged from his reflection upon the Psalms (Acts 1:20), and then the explosion of scriptural insights he unleashed on the crowd at Pentecost (Acts 2:16–41). Isn't it likely that the Holy Spirit had been bringing key points of that first sermon to Peter's consciousness throughout the nine days of prayer?

When we pray the Rosary today, when we recite the *Hail Mary while meditating on the events recounted in the gospels and Acts* (the twenty Mysteries), we enter into the Apostles' experience. "With the Rosary, the Christian people sits at the school of Mary and is led to contemplate the beauty on the face of Christ and to experience the depths of his love."[6] And by doing this regularly, daily, our souls grow and become progressively more docile to the movement of the Holy Spirit. We receive not one, but several Pentecosts, as our eyes open up onto new spiritual vistas and we find ourselves acting with a freedom and strength we imagined ourselves unable to attain— and rightly so; these things can only take root in souls that have been broken up and seeded, over time, through prayer. These souls are made ready for that moment when the Living Water rains down and causes new life to burst forth into the open.

Jesus knows how we are made, and he knows how to remake us in his image; that was why he sent the Apostles back to the upper room. They needed to spend that time in prayer, in meditation . . . in the company of his mother. Almost 2,000 years may have passed, but the prescription remains the same. That is why, when Jesus sends our Lady to earth, she so often asks that we pray the Rosary. Outside of the Mass, it combines more prayer forms than any other devotion we have considered: the Creed (the Church's *Shema*), the *Our Father*, the communion of saints, vocal prayer, petition, and meditation on Scripture. Also, as with the psalms in the Temple, it is traditional to pray different sets of mysteries on different days. Here is a handy chart giving Scripture verses you can read at the start of each meditation along with the day each is traditionally prayed:

6. Ibid., no. 1.

Mysteries of the Rosary

Joyful	Luminous	Sorrowful	Glorious
Annunciation (Luke 1:26–33, 38)	*Baptism of Jesus* (Mark 1:9–13)	*Agony in Garden* (Luke 23:39–46)	*Resurrection* (Mark 16:1–7; John 20:1–18)
Visitation (Luke 1:39–45)	*Wedding Feast of Cana* (John 2:1–11)	*Scourging at Pillar* (Mark 15:6–15)	*Ascension* (Luke 24:46–53)
Nativity (Luke 2:6–12)	*Jesus's Proclamation of the Kingdom* (Matt. 4:17, 23–25)	*Crowning with Thorns* (John 19:1–8)	*Descent of Holy Spirit* (Acts 2:1–7)
Presentation (Luke 2:25–35)	*Transfiguration* (Luke 9:28–36)	*Carrying the Cross* (John 19:16–22; Luke 23:26–31)	*Assumption of Mary* (Rev. 11:19–12:2)
Finding in Temple (Luke 2:41–50)	*Institution of Eucharist* (Luke 22:14–20)	*Crucifixion* (John 19:25–30).	*Coronation of Mary* (Rev. 12:1–2; 2 Tim. 4:8)
Monday & Saturday	**Thursday**	**Tuesday & Friday**	**Wed. & Sunday**

You're of course free to pray any set of mysteries on any day—or to pray all twenty mysteries in the course of the same day. You don't have to limit your meditations to these events, either; you can branch out to other events in Scripture. The important thing is that, with Mary, you treasure Christ's words and deeds in your heart (Luke 2:51).

The Rosary is such an incredible form of prayer. By praying the *Hail Mary* as we meditate, our lips are forming the words of Scripture at the same time our hearts and minds ponder it. And we're invoking the woman in whom the Word took flesh to pray that he becomes so in us, too!

12

Christ in You,
The Hope of Glory

Christ enables us to live in him *all that he himself lived, and* he lives it in us. . . . *We must continue to accomplish in ourselves the stages of Jesus's life and his mysteries.* CCC 521

✝

AT THE TRANSFIGURATION, the eyes of Peter, James, and John were finally allowed to register the divine life pouring through Jesus's humanity. I hope these past eleven chapters have helped you to understand the Church's teaching that Jesus now pours himself out to the Father through his Church, through *your life and prayer*. I hope that, like me, you stand in awe of the myriad ways the Church's sacraments, devotions, and practices let us *participate* in his prayer. We pray with him in the home at Nazareth, in the synagogue and in the Temple, in the desert and on the mountains, in Gethsemane and at the Cross; and in him we even approach our Father in heaven.

How Has This Worked Out in My Life?

It is a fair question. If a person writes a book like this, then he should at least have the decency to come clean about his prayer life. First, let me say that I do not regularly practice all of the devotions discussed in these pages. If you want to build a successful exercise regimen, you do not begin by committing to go to the gym an hour a day, every day; it would be too much of a shock to your body and to your schedule. Rather, you start slow, with an activity you enjoy (or can tolerate) for a short amount of time, and you gradually add to it. It is sensible advice for advancing in prayer, too.

Like most people, my mornings consist of a lot of multi-tasking. I make the Sign of the Cross as I roll out of bed. If it is a morning that I work out, then I do steps on the Wii-Fit as I use my iPod to pray the Liturgy of the Hours. I wear the Brown Scapular of Our Lady of Mt. Carmel, and when I remove it to shower or put it back on, I pray, "Jesus, please clothe me and my family in your mother's prayers for our salvation." In the shower I pray the Creed and *Our Father* and then ask Mary and Joseph to intercede with me for family and friends. When I return to my bedroom to finish getting ready, I flip on the computer and check for new emails. I always try to open God's first. (The Daily Gospel is kind enough to send Mass readings for the day. You can subscribe at www.dailygospel.org.)

After I've herded the children into the car and leave for school, we have a three-minute prayer time. One of them starts out by thanking God for all the ways he takes care of us and asks his blessing on our family and on anything that worries us. We make a morning offering: "Jesus, we want to offer you our entire day through the heart of your mother, Mary—all our thoughts, words, actions, joys, sorrows, and frustrations. We pray that you take them all, Lord, and offer them to your heavenly Father in union with your own sacrifice, made present for us in the Eucharist. Please bring us safely to heaven one day." The summit of our morning prayer is the *Our Father*, which we follow with the *Hail Mary* and a short litany of saints. It is nothing fancy, but it grounds us before the daily grind sets in.

Once I drop my children off at school, I grab the Rosary off of the rearview mirror. Praying the Rosary on my commute to work is the meat and potatoes of my daily prayer; those twenty to thirty minutes feed my soul. (On vacation days I take the Rosary with me as I walk.) Jesus's life is an inexhaustible source of meditation, and it gives me a chance to listen for God's voice. The inspiration for at least half of what I write or share in talks pops into my head during the Rosary.

When I arrive at work, I get busy doing speech and language therapy. In the course of the day there are a lot of things for which to thank Jesus, as well as petitions to offer up to him. On the way home I pray the chaplet of Divine Mercy. (I drive home around dinner time, but I figure it's three o'clock somewhere.)

At home the children and I pray at dinner and also when I tuck them in, but most of our time is spent doing run-of-the-mill things. We do homework, play games, and watch TV. We're fortunate to have "holy reminders" around the house, especially an image of the Sacred Heart enthroned in the living room. God uses them to catch my attention. I am reminded of his love, reminded to thank him or ask his help, or subtly reminded to change my attitude. The holy cards taped behind the kitchen sink—of the Holy Family and St. Michael the Archangel—are great reminders to ask their prayers for my family and home. The amazing thing is that, even when my children and I are focused on doing something and not specifically thinking about the Lord, the Holy Spirit and our morning offering turn our activity into prayer.

When I climb into bed at night, I spend a few minutes of quiet time with the Lord. Most nights I read from one of the gospels. Some nights I use my iPod to join in Night Prayer from the Liturgy of the Hours. And there are those occasional nights when I just fall into bed thanking Jesus for the day, confessing my sins, and asking him to help me tomorrow.

The most important element of my prayer life is the Eucharist. It is Jesus; it is his Passover. I offer myself with him upon the altar, and when I receive him in Communion, I ask the Holy Spirit to unite my soul to Mary's, to fill it with all of her love and adoration of Jesus. On my way home from work, I am sometimes able to stop and visit Jesus in eucharistic adoration. I may only be able to stay for five minutes, but it's a chance to be in his presence and tell him that I love him. I hope those visits make reparation for the many ways I fail him.

Do I have room to grow? Of course I do; prior to heaven we all do. But that is no reason for discouragement. Through the Church, Jesus has given us all of these amazing practices and prayer forms, and chief among them he's given us the sacraments. But at the heart of Christian prayer is the stupendous reality that the person who has poured himself out to the Father from all eternity, who became flesh to teach us about prayer, who spent countless hours in prayer, and has taken human prayer to its ultimate height in his crucifixion, resurrection, and ascension, *lives inside of us*! It is the great mystery—"Christ in you, the hope of glory" (Col. 1:27). And if we cooperate with him, then the God who began this great work of prayer in us will see it through to completion (Phil. 1:6).

The important thing is to begin. Attending the Sunday Eucharist and having at least one daily time of prayer that includes the *Our Father* are the absolute prerequisites. Unite yourself to Jesus every morning and ask him to make all your thoughts, words, and actions a gift to the Father. Accept the challenge to try one other practice or devotion recommended here for at least a week. If it is a good fit, then commit to using it for a month. Whatever the practice is, recognize that it is Jesus offering himself to the Father *through you*. You, my friend, are being inserted into the very life of the Trinity!

> Through him, and with him, and in him, O God, almighty Father, in the unity of the Holy Spirit, all glory and honor is yours, forever and ever. Amen.[1]

1. *Roman Missal*, 3rd ed., Doxology.

Appendix I

Comparing the *Our Father*
and Eighteen Benedictions

THE FOLLOWING INCLUDES my thoughts on how the Eighteen Bene-dictions can be viewed as being encapsulated in the seven petitions of the *Our Father*.

The *Our Father*	The Eighteen Benedictions
	"Blessed be the Lord…"
Our Father, Who art in heaven, hallowed be Thy Name	1) …the God of Abraham, Isaac, and Jacob, our shield through the ages. 3) …the only God. 15) …who hears our prayers. 17) …whom it is right to thank. Thank You for the mercy, kindness, and goodness You have shown to us, and our fathers and mothers before us.
Thy kingdom come	2) …who raises the dead. 12) …who humbles the arrogant, the heretics. Remove them from among Your people. 14) …who rebuilt Jerusalem. Restore the kingdom of David, Your anointed one.
Thy will be done on earth as it is in heaven	11) …who loves justice. Give us wise judges and leaders, as we had in times past. 18) …who creates peace. Give Your peace to Your people Israel.
Give us this day our daily bread	4) …who gives knowledge. Give us understanding of Your Law. 8) …who heals the sick. Heal the pain in our hearts. 9) …who blesses the yearly harvest. Send our lands all they need to be fruitful. 13) …who shelters the righteous. Shower goodness upon converts and reward all who do Your will. 16) …who allows us to worship in His sanctuary. May He always dwell in Jerusalem.
Forgive us our tres-passes as we forgive those we trespass against us	6) …who forgives. Forgive us our sins against You.
Lead us not into temptation	5) …who loves repentance. Make us turn back to You. 10) …who gathers the exiles of Israel. Bring them back.
But deliver us from evil.	7) …who has redeemed Israel. Save us from our enemies.

Appendix II
Why Call God "Father" Instead of "Mother"?

MANY WITHIN OUR CULTURE question why God cannot be addressed as "Mother" instead of "Father." The underlying assumption in this question is that Jesus's choice of Father was culturally conditioned. The difficulty with that assumption is the freedom Jesus demonstrated throughout his ministry in breaking with the gender conventions of the time: meeting with women privately, welcoming them to travel with him independent of their husbands, and his selection of women, unable to testify in courts of law, to act as the first witnesses to his resurrection. His decision to name only males as apostles and address God with the masculine "Father" was not circumscribed by the culture. In fact, priestesses and female deities existed throughout the Middle East as well as among the Greeks and Romans. As the Word made flesh, Jesus's revelation of God as Father was free and deliberate—but why?

In Hebrew and Christian thought, God is bigger than gender. *Both* male and female are reflections of the Deity (Gen. 1:27). Scripture *compares* God to a mother (Isa. 49:15; Hos. 11:3–4). And yet, throughout the whole of Scripture, God is never *addressed* as "Mother." There is something about fatherhood that is more analogous than motherhood to describing God's relationship to us. Scripture does not come out and explain it, but I would suggest that male and female have been invested by God with an "iconic character." By this, I mean that the difference we observe between male and female can give us insight into spiritual realities.

Think about the complementary roles the mother and father play in the conception of the child. The father comes from the "outside," while the mother welcomes him into herself. The ovum produced by the mother awaits the father's sperm cell, and the union of

138

the two produces the child's body. The child then grows within his mother, unable to see his father's face until birth. God also plays a "fatherly" role in every conception—coming from *outside of all creation* to breathe a spirit, an intellectual soul, *a heart* into the child at the instant of his/her conception. All of God's actions come from "the outside" so to speak, and in this way are fatherly. The Church, on the other hand—and the individual souls that make it up—is the part of creation that has received God into itself and allowed Him to bring forth new supernatural life. In this analogy, whether biologically male or female, each human soul resembles the feminine. This would explain why Scripture refers to the Church as Christ's Bride (Eph. 5:22–23) and the Mother of the faithful (Rev. 12:17).

As we have said throughout this work, our goal is to pray through, with, and in Jesus. *In union with him* we say, "Our Father, who art in heaven."

Appendix III
Twelve Promises Attached
to the Sacred Heart Devotion

THE FOLLOWING are the most well-known of the promises recorded by St. Margaret Mary Alacoque. They call attention to the great promises made to us in Scripture.

Those who practice devotion to the Sacred Heart:	Statements in Scripture
1. Will receive all the graces necessary for their state of life.	Matt. 6:33; Phil. 1:5–6
2. Will have peace in their families.	Acts 2:38–39; John 10:9
3. Will have Jesus's consolation in all their troubles.	John 14:18, 21
4. Will experience Jesus as their refuge in life and especially in death.	John 14:27, 3
5. Will be abundantly blessed in all they undertake.	Luke 11:9–10
6. Sinners will find an infinite ocean of mercy.	John 6:37, 7:37
7. The lukewarm will become fervent.	Matt. 11:28
8. The fervent will speed to great perfection.	Matt. 12:50
9. Jesus will bless places where the image of his Sacred Heart is exposed and venerated.	Rev. 21:3
10. Priests will touch the most hardened hearts.	Exod. 4:12; Luke 12:12; Rev. 3:20
11. Those who spread the devotion will have their names written on Jesus's Heart for eternity.	Rev. 3:21; Isa. 49:16
12. Those who receive Communion on the first Fridays of nine consecutive months will receive, before death, the grace of final repentance and the sacraments.	John 3:16, 5:24, 6:54

Bibliography

Benedict XVI. *Jesus of Nazareth: From the Baptism in the Jordan to the Transfiguration*. New York: Doubleday, 2007.

Cantalamessa, Raniero. *The Holy Spirit in the Life of Jesus*. Collegeville, MN: The Liturgical Press, 1994.

Catechism of the Catholic Church. 2nd ed. Vatican City: Libreria Editrice Vaticana, 1997.

Clark, Steven B. *Introduction to the Eucharist*. Ann Arbor, MI: Servant Publications, 2000.

Croiset, Jean. *The Devotion to the Sacred Heart of Jesus*. Rockford, IL: TAN Books and Publishers, Inc., 1988.

De Montfort, Louis Marie. *True Devotion to the Blessed Virgin*. Bay Shore, NY: Montfort Publications, 1996.

DiSante, Carmine. *Jewish Prayer: The Origins of the Christian Liturgy*. Mahwah, NJ: Paulist Press, 1991.

Edersheim, Alfred. *Sketches of Jewish Social Life*. New York: James Pott & Co., 1881.

Finkel, Asher. "Prayer in Jewish Life of the First Century." In *Into God's Presence: Prayer in the New Testament*, edited by Richard N. Longenecker. Grand Rapids, MI: Wm. B. Eerdmans Publishing Co., 2001.

Fitzmeyer, Joseph A. *Luke: The Anchor Bible: v. 28–28a*. New York: Doubleday, 1985.

France, R.T. *Jesus and the Old Testament*. Vancouver, British Columbia: Regent College Publishing, 1998.

General Instruction of the Liturgy of the Hours. No.33. Congregation for Divine Worship, February 2, 1971. http://www.ewtn.com/library/curia/cdwgilh.htm.

Gertrude the Great: Herald of Divine Love. Rockford, IL: TAN Books and Publishers, Inc., 1989.

Grant, Frederick C. *Ancient Judaism and the New Testament*. New York: The Macmillan Co., 1959.

Gray, Timothy. *Reading Scripture for a Change: An Introduction to Lectio Divina*. West Chester, PA: Ascension Press, 2009.

Grelot, P., and J. Pierron. *The Paschal Feast in the Bible*. Baltimore: Helicon, 1966.

Groeschel, Benedict, and James Monti. *In the Presence of Our Lord: The*

History, Theology, and Psychology of Eucharistic Devotion. Huntington, IN: Our Sunday Visitor, Inc., 1997.

Hahn, Scott. *The Lamb's Supper: The Mass as Heaven on Earth.* New York: Doubleday, 1999.

——. *Understanding "Our Father": Biblical Reflections on the Lord's Prayer.* Steubenville, OH: Emmaus Road Publishing, 2002.

Haring, Bernard. *Heart of Jesus: Symbol of Redeeming Love.* Liguori, MO: Liguori Publications, 1983.

Harrington, Daniel J. *Jesus and Prayer: What the New Testament Teaches Us.* Ijamsville, MD: The Word Among Us Press, 2009.

Heinemann, Joseph. *Prayer in the Talmud: Forms and Patterns.* Berlin-New York: de Gruyter, 1977.

——. and Jakob J. Petuchowski, eds. *Literature of the Synagogue.* New York: Behrman House, 1975.

Hinnebusch, Paul. *The Lord's Prayer in the Light of Our Lord's Life and Preaching.* Boston: Pauline Books & Media, 1996.

Jeremias, Joachim. *The Prayers of Jesus.* Naperville, IL: Alec R. Allenson, Inc., 1967.

Jones, Michael Keenan. *Toward a Theology of Christ the High Priest.* Rome: Editrice Pontifica Universita Gregoriana, 2006.

Jurgens, William A. *The Faith of the Early Fathers.* Vol. 1. Collegeville, MN: The Liturgical Press, 1970.

Kaiser, William. *The Uses of the Old Testament in the New.* Chicago: Moody Press, 1985.

Kapler, Shane. *The God Who Is Love: Explaining Christianity from Its Center.* St. Louis: Out of the Box, 2009.

Kodell, Jerome. *The Eucharist in the New Testament.* Collegeville, MN: The Liturgical Press, 1988.

Kowalska, Mary Faustina. *Diary: Divine Mercy in My Soul.* Stockbridge, MA: Marians of the Immaculate Conception, 1996.

Larkin, Francis. *Enthronement of the Sacred Heart.* Boston: Daughters of St. Paul, 1978.

Lomask, Milton. *The Curé of Ars: The Priest Who Outtalked the Devil.* New York: Vision Books, 1966.

Lucia, Sister. *"Calls" from the Message of Fatima.* Still River, MA: Ravengate Press, 2005.

Maertens, Thierry. *Bible Themes: A Source Book.* Vol. II. Notre Dame: Fides/Claretian, 1964.

Manns, Frederic. *Jewish Prayer in the Time of Jesus.* Jerusalem: Franciscan Printing Press, 1994.

Bibliography

Meier, John. *A Marginal Jew: Rethinking the Historical Jesus.* Vol. 2. New York: Doubleday, 1994.

O'Donnell, Timothy. *The Heart of the Redeemer.* San Francisco: Ignatius Press, 1992.

Pitre, Brant. "Was Jesus Really Crucified with the Passover Lambs?" http://www.thesacredpage.com/2010/04/jewish-roots-of-jesus-passion-and-death.html.

Rahner, Hugo. "On the Biblical Basis of the Devotion." In *Heart of the Saviour,* edited by Josef Stierli. New York: Herder and Herder, 1957.

Ratzinger, Joseph. *Behold the Pierced One: An Approach to a Spiritual Christology.* Ignatius Press: San Francisco, 1986.

————. *The Feast of Faith.* San Francisco: Ignatius Press, 1986.

————. *The God of Jesus Christ.* San Francisco: Ignatius Press, 2008.

————. *The Spirit of the Liturgy.* San Francisco: Ignatius Press, 2000.

Ritmeyer, Leen, and Kathleen Ritmeyer. *The Ritual of the Temple in the Time of Christ.* Jerusalem: Carta, 2002.

Saward, John. *Redeemer in the Womb.* San Francisco: Ignatius Press, 1993.

Sheed, Frank. *To Know Christ Jesus.* San Francisco: Ignatius Press, 1980.

Smith, Barry D. *Jesus's Last Passover Meal.* Lewiston, NY: Mellen Biblical Press, 1993.

Vivian, Benedict. "The Gospel According to Matthew." In *The New Jerome Biblical Commentary,* edited by R.E. Brown, J.A. Fitzmeyer, and R.E. Murphy. Englewood Cliffs, NJ: Prentice Hall, 1990.

Whiston, William. *Josephus: The Complete Works.* Dallas: Thomas Nelson, 1998.

Wiesel, Elie, and Mark Podwal. *A Passover Haggadah.* New York: Simon & Schuster, Inc., 1993.

Wolfer, Vianney. *The Prayer of Christ According to the Teaching of St. Thomas Aquinas.* Washington: Catholic University of America Press, 1958.

Wylen, Stephen M. *The Jews in the Time of Jesus: An Introduction.* Mawah, NJ: Paulist Press, 1995.

Made in the USA
Monee, IL
24 February 2022

91781382R00100